Physical Characteristics of the Shiba Inu

(from the American Kennel Club breed standard)

Topline: Straight and level to the base of the tail.

Tail: Thick and powerful and is carried over the back in a sickle or curled position. A loose single curl or sickle tail pointing vigorously toward the neck and nearly parallel to the back is preferred. In length the tail reaches nearly to the hock joint when extended. Tail is set high.

Hindquarters: The angulation of the hindquarters is moderate and in balance with the angulation of the forequarters. Hind legs are strong with a wide natural stance. The hock joint is strong, turning neither in nor out. Upper thighs are long and the second thighs short but well developed.

Color: All colors are clear and intense. The undercoat is cream, buff or gray.
Bright orange-red with urajiro. Clear red preferred but a very slight dash of black tipping is permitted on the back and tail.
Black with tan points and urajiro. Black hairs have a brownish cast, not blue. The borderline between black and tan areas is clearly defined.
Sesame (black-tipped hairs on a rich red background) with urajiro. Tipping is light and even on the body and head with no concentration of black in any area.

Body: Dry and well muscled without the appearance of sluggishness or coarseness. Abdomen is firm and well tucked-up. Back is firm.

Size: Males 14.5 inches to 16.5 inches at withers. Females 13.5 inches to 15.5 inches. The preferred size is the middle of the range for each sex. Average weight at preferred size is approximately 23 pounds for males, 17 pounds for females.

Feet: Catlike with well-arched toes fitting tightly together. Pads are thick.

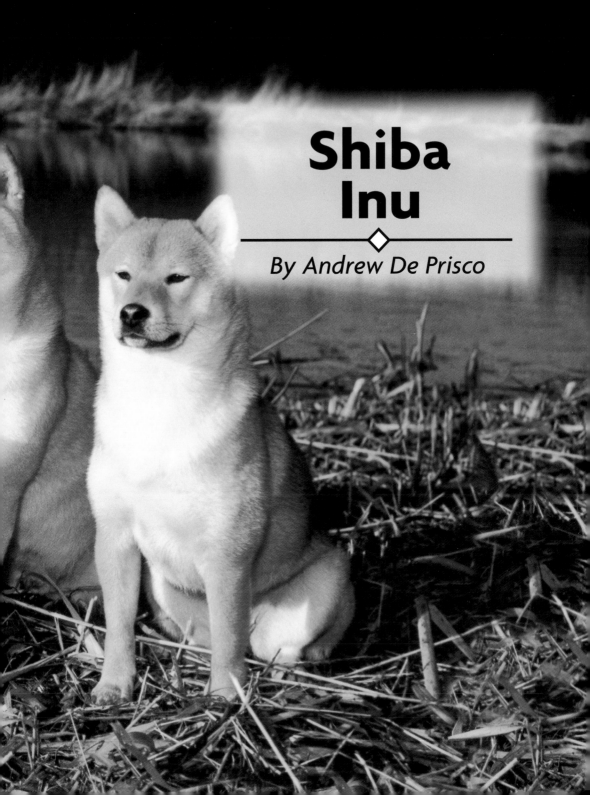

Shiba Inu

◇

By Andrew De Prisco

Contents

Training Your Shiba Inu   90

Begin with the basics of training the puppy and adult dog. Learn the principles of house-training the Shiba Inu, including the use of crates and basic scent instincts. Enter Puppy Kindergarten and introduce the pup to his collar and leash and progress to the basic commands. Find out about obedience classes and other activities.

Healthcare for Your Shiba Inu   113

By Lowell Ackerman DVM, DACVD
Become your dog's healthcare advocate and a well-educated canine keeper. Select a skilled and able veterinarian. Discuss pet insurance, vaccinations and infectious diseases, the neuter/spay decision and a sensible, effective plan for parasite control, including fleas, ticks and worms.

Showing Your Shiba Inu   142

Step into the center ring and find out about the world of showing pure-bred dogs. Here's how to get started in AKC shows, how they are organized and what's required for your dog to become a champion.

Behavior of Your Shiba Inu   148

Analyze the canine mind to understand what makes your Shiba Inu tick. The following potential problems are addressed: aggression, separation anxiety, sexual misconduct, chewing, digging and food-related problems.

KENNEL CLUB BOOKS® **SHIBA INU**
ISBN 13: 978-1-59378-276-4

Copyright © 2004 • Kennel Club Books® • A Division of BowTie, Inc.
40 Main Street, Freehold, NJ 07728 USA
Cover Design Patented: US 6,435,559 B2 • Printed in South Korea

Photography by Isabelle Français
with additional photos by:

Ashbey Photography, Mary Bloom, Paulette Braun, T.J. Calhoun, Alan and Sandy Carey, Carolina Biological Supply, Tom DiGiacomo, Carol Ann Johnson, Bill Jonas, Dr. Dennis Kunkel, Tam C. Nguyen, Phototake, Jean Claude Revy, Karen Taylor and Alice van Kempen.

Illustrations by Patricia Peters.

The author dedicates this book to his first two Shibas, the ever-smiling Kabuki and the wondrous, immortal Tengu, both missed dearly every day.

Author Andrew De Prisco, a prolific writer and editor of dog books, with his ever-smiling, ever-loving bitch Kabuki.

HISTORY OF THE

SHIBA INU

Isolated from intruders from across the sea, Japan basked in virtual independence for centuries. This highly ritualistic society, rather primitive compared to the Western world, with which it had very little contact until the latter half of the 19th century, was content to pass on its history and culture without interruption.

The nation's indigenous dogs, regarded today as "Natural Monuments," are mostly members of the spitz family, including the Akita, Shiba, Kai and many others. Spitz dogs derive from the colder climates and possess characteristic features that facilitate their survival in sub-zero conditions. Well-furred, erect and small ears protect the dog from wind and snow; a dense double coat provides insulation from the cold as well as coolness from heat, should the need arise; a well-furnished, tightly curled tail covers the dog's nose when he is sleeping in his typical circular position; a wolf-like muzzle warms the air through the long passages

before entering the animal's lungs. From the tiny Shiba to the giant Akita, all the Japanese spitz breeds share these essential physical characteristics.

The Shiba, the smallest of Japan's spitz breeds, possesses all of these traits, plus a ton of personality and attitude. Among the Shiba's cousins are the Akita, the largest and most popular of these indigenous spitzes; the Ainu, or Hokkaido, a fearless guard dog; and three other middle-sized dogs, the Shikoku, Kai and Kishu. Of these six Japanese breeds, only the Shiba and Akita have established followings outside Japan, although the other four are recognized by the Fédération Cynologique Internationale (FCI), the world kennel club association. The breed known as the Japanese Spitz is not related to the Shiba but to the Samoyed, in whose image the breed was created. Americans recognize the similarities between the Japanese Spitz and the Miniature American Eskimo Dog, also a solid white, abundantly coated Nordic dog.

The largest spitz breed of Japan, the Akita enjoys world-wide popularity, despite the unfortunate politics that have divided the breed into the Japanese Akita and the American Akita, also recognized as the Great Japanese Dog.

To Westerners, the notion of a small, efficiently built dynamo from Japan is an apparently modern one. However, history reveals that the Shiba Inu is much older than the Toyota Corolla or the Honda Accord, and goes even farther per gallon of gas! Archeologists in Japan have unearthed the remains of small dogs with curled tails dating back to 8000 BC. Experts assert that these diminutive but sturdily built skeletons represent the ancestors of the Shiba Inu. Based on pottery from the Jomon Period (8000 to 200 BC), these small dogs were used by men to hunt deer, boar and bear. Most scholars agree that the Shiba Inu is the oldest and purest of the Japanese spitz breeds.

Shibas could be found in various regions of Japan, differing slightly in coloration, coat length and density, bone and maturation. These variations can still be seen in Shibas today, though breeders have strived to agree upon and establish one correct type. From the mountainous regions, the Shibas bred for hunting possessed heavier bone and coarser type. Colors varied from region to region: e.g., the intense red coloration of the San-In region dogs compared to the mottled black coloration of the Yamanashi region dogs. The Shin-Shu and Mino type dogs were smaller in size and lighter

TEN BREEDS OF JAPAN

There are ten Japanese breeds recognized by the Japan Kennel Club (JKC) and the Fédération Cynologique Internationale (FCI). The Japanese spitz breeds are divided by size, namely the Akita as the largest breed; the Shiba as the smallest breed, and four medium-size breeds, Kai, Kishu, Shikoku and Ainu (or Hokkaido). Only the Akita and Shiba have established significant followings outside Japan. There are four other recognized Japanese breeds, including the giant mastiff breed known as the Tosa, the lovely toy breed known as the Chin, the solid white Japanese Spitz and the diminutive Japanese Terrier. Of course, the Chin is the most popular of these breeds worldwide. In Japan, the Shiba is the most popular Japanese breed, followed by the Japanese Spitz, Chin and Akita.

in bone, prized for their hunting prowess and boundless energy. The Mino Shibas possessed the darkest red coloration, the color preferred by most Shiba fanciers today, as well as dark brown triangular eyes, thick ears and a sickle tail (compared to the curled tail of the other Shiba types).

COLORS IN JAPANESE SHIBAS

Burning with the fire of the Japanese sun, the red Shiba Inu has become the most prized of the Shiba colors, though it is by no means the only recognized or desirable Shiba color. There are three colors in the Shiba: red, red sesame and black and tan. Some controversy existed over other colors, including white (which is acceptable in other Japanese breeds but not Shibas) as well as gray and brindle (both of which are seen in other Japanese breeds but do not exist in Shibas). The sesame color is created by a combination of black and white hairs with the principal color red. The term "urajiro" describes the desirable white coat markings on the Shiba's muzzle, neck and lower jaw, cheeks, chest, stomach, underside of tail and inside of legs. All three coat colors should have white in these areas.

While the breed standard of

CANIS LUPUS

"Grandma, what big teeth you have!" The gray wolf, a familiar figure in fairy tales and legends, has had its reputation tarnished and its population pummeled over the centuries. Yet it is the descendants of this much-feared creature to which we open our homes and hearts. Our beloved dog, *Canis domesticus,* derives directly from the gray wolf, a highly social canine that lives in elaborately structured packs. In the wild, the gray wolf can range from 60 to 175 pounds, standing between 25 and 40 inches in height.

the American Kennel Club lists the breed's three correct colors, the English Kennel Club's interim standard lists "red, black, black and tan or brindle. White with red or gray tinge" as correct Shiba colors. The brindle pattern is associated not with the Shiba but with its

The Ainu, or Hokkaido, originated in the northern Japanese island called Hokkaido. The breed is somewhat larger than the Shiba and used as a hunting and companion dog.

cousin the Kai, "the Tiger Dog," which can be found in red, black and gray brindles. White is frowned upon in the breed's native Japan and is associated with the Kishu, not the Shiba. There is no mention of the red sesame coloration—a pity! As for a solid black Shiba?... perhaps some club member owned a black and tan without the tan and lobbied for its inclusion in the standard. A puzzlement, to say the least! A later version of The English Kennel Club standard lists red,

The Shikoku is one of the Japanese native spitz breeds that is medium in size. Like fellow medium-sized spitz breeds, the breed is rarely seen outside Japan.

A black and tan Japanese Shiba bitch, showing ideal markings and an alert stance.

red sesame, black and tan, and white, with descriptions of each.

Color prejudice and politics abound in many breeds. It is sad to see that the show scene in the UK and US has become so partial to red Shibas that black and tan and red sesame exhibits are practically non-existent. The Shiba has never been a one-color breed and this author, who favors the truly unique Japanese color, red sesame, patiently awaits the turn of the trend when exhibitors can enter the ring with a red sesame (or black and tan!) and have an equal chance at the blue ribbons.

BREED NAME

In the Japanese language, words have various meanings, similar to the concept of homonyms in the English language. Thus the word *shiba* in Japanese has a variety of meanings. Some say that *shiba* refers to the red coloration of dried brushwood (called shiba), recognizing that the Shiba has also been called the Brushwood Dog. Others state that *shiba* simply means "small," as the breed has been called the Japanese Small Dog in some English text books.

Unlike the Shiba, the other Japanese breeds have been named for their regions, such as the Akita, Sanshu and Hokkaido, all of which are named for the locality in which the breed originated. Because the Shiba is associated with

A solid-white Akita is less common than other colors, though it is perfectly acceptable and handsome.

The Ainu, or Hokkaido, comes in colors similar to the Shiba, including this black and tan pattern.

"Urajiro" refers to the white markings on the Shiba's coat, seen on this red sesame on its neck, muzzle, cheeks and chest.

This black and tan Japanese Shiba is smiling about its newfound popularity in the Western world, even if its red brethren are favored by most fanciers (and judges).

numerous regions, various names for Shiba types have evolved. The Shin-Shu Shiba derived from Nagano, the central mountainous area of Honshu, and is perhaps the most famous of the Shiba types. Other names include the Mino Shiba (from Gifu Prefecture) and the San-In Shiba (from Tottori and Shimane Prefectures and the northwestern part of Honshu).

The words *inu* and *ken* in Japanese simply translate as "dog." It is not uncommon for the breed to be called Shiba Inu or Shiba Ken. This suffix can be used with any of the Japanese breed names, such as Sanshu Inu or Akita Ken.

WESTERN INFLUENCE ON JAPAN

In the mid-1850s, Commodore Matthew Perry and the US Navy pried open Japanese ports and forced the Japanese to see how "behind the times" their semi-feudal society indeed was. Among the Western imports that helped "modernize" Japan were the popular European dog breeds, including German Shepherd Dogs, Poodles and Dachshunds as well as many gundog breeds, such as Pointers and English Setters, igniting a new trend for hunting in Japan. Among the upper-class fanciers, these Western breeds were prized for their specialized skills and "foreignness," and the native Japanese breeds were neglected for decades or crossbred haphazardly to the imported dogs.

NATIVE BREEDS OF JAPAN

BREED	SIZE	COLORS	UTILITY
Shiba	13.5-16.5 in	Red, red sesame, black and tan	Small bird hunting/companion
Shikoku	17-22 in	White, fawn, tan, gray, pied	Deer hunting/companion
Sanshu	16-22 in	Fawn, red, black & tan, tan, salt & pepper or pied	Guarding/companion
Kai	18-23 in	Black brindle, red brindle, brindle	Deer hunting
Kishu	17-22 in	White	Herding/guarding
Hokkaido/Ainu	18-22 in	Red, fawn, black & tan	Bear and deer hunting/guarding
Akita	24-28 in	Any including brindle or pinto	Bear and boar hunting/guarding

This influx of Western breeds nearly caused the extinction of the pure Japanese breeds, including the Shiba. It was not until 1928 when Dr Hiroyoshi Saito formed a club dedicated to the preservation of these native Japanese breeds that the situation began to rectify itself. The new organization, known as the Nihon Ken Kozonkai (for short, Nippo), was successful in persuading the Japanese government to designate the native breeds as "Natural Monuments" in the 1930s under the Cultural Properties Act. The Shiba breed was designated in 1936.

Nippo drafted breed standards for the native breeds, held shows for native breeds and registered dogs. Tako was the first Shiba to be registered and was the only Shiba of the

"URAJIRO"

This Japanese word refers to the white (or cream) coloration on the coat of the Shiba. These markings are on the side of the nose, cheeks, beneath the jaw and neck, chest, abdomen and insides of the legs. Some Shibas also have white markings on their legs, giving the impression of socks, though these are not required on American Shibas.

15 entered in the first Nippo show to be "recommended" for type. Of course, breed type in all six breeds was variable at best, as there were few good examples of the breeds left in most areas. Interest in the breeds grew in Japan, though not overseas, and more shows and clubs were formed in Japan. The national Nippo show of 1939 saw Aka of Fugoku, a ten-month-old Shiba dog, winning the major award, which had previously only been won by the larger breeds. Aka and his offspring would survive the oncoming Second World War and become the foundation of the modern Shiba.

Due to the breed's recogni-

tion as a "Natural Monument," the FCI recognized the Shiba, and dogs were shown in major shows in Tokyo. World War II dealt a devastating blow to all dog activities in Japan, and the Shiba nearly became extinct. The San-In and Mino Shibas were harder hit than the Shin-Shu Shibas. Following the war, an outbreak of distemper in 1959 caused further damage to the surviving Shiba strains. Breeders had to rescue the breed by recreating breeding programs, transporting dogs from the montane regions to urban centers. The remaining dogs from various lines were combined to create the foundation of today's Shibas. Breeders were forced to select sires and

MOST INFLUENTIAL RESTORATION SHIBAS

NAME	SIRE	DAM
Ishi	Hisahara	Kochi
Koro	Unknown	Unknown
Aka of Fugoku	Ishi	Koro
Naka of Akaishiso	Akani	Beniko
Nakaichi of Akaishiso	Naka	Beniko
Tenko of Jonenso	Senko	Tamahime
Matsumaru of Shinshu	Benisachi	Aka Fusame
Meiho of Shimamura	Koronaka	Eienme
Kuratanoishi of Kurataso	Ichiroku	Korohime
Hideyoshi of Shinshu Kirinso	Benisachi	Umehime
Taketoyo of Hokoso	Meiho Kenikomo no Tetsu	Kuro Yakko

NIPPO IN THE BUDDING

The organization known as Nippo, formally Nihon Ken Kozonkai, was founded in 1928. In English, the formal name translates to "organization to preserve Japanese dogs." The first of the Nippo shows in Japan were also held in 1928.

Japanese society was unstable and anxious, in part due to the change in the recognized value system of the nation. Many Japanese families sought the protection of German Shepherds or other guard-dog-type breeds that they encountered from the occupational forces living in Japan. In time, the Japanese realized that they needed an organization to help regulate the breeding of these dogs, and the All Japan Guard Dog Association (AJGDA) was formed in 1948 with Kijuro Shidehara serving as honorary chairman and Tanzan Ishibashi as chairman. This organization was the predecessor of the Japan Kennel Club. The first show for the AJGDA was held

dams from the dwindling Shiba population—dogs of known and pure origins—or to crossbreed to a similar Japanese dog known as the Mikawa. The Mikawa has been discredited for being crossbred with the Shiba to recreate the breed. Some Mikawas were even passed off as Shibas. The Mikawa possessed uncharacteristic round eyes and lacked the desired "urajiro" markings, sure signs of mixed breeding with Western breeds. The Mikawa lost favor in Japan and is no longer registered by the JKC or FCI. Most breeders opted not to include the Mikawa in their programs, and resultant health problems ensued due to the limited gene pool. The occurrence of slipped kneecaps and missing teeth still plagues Shiba breeders today.

JAPANESE DEVELOPMENT IN THE 20TH CENTURY

Following the devastation of the Second World War,

The modern Shiba is a typy, noble small dog with characteristic almond-shaped eyes, small ears and a spitz tail.

PURE-BRED PURPOSE
Given the vast range of the world's 400 or so pure breeds of dog, it's fair to say that domestic dogs are the most versatile animal in the kingdom. From the tiny 1-pound lap dog to the 200-pound guard dog, dogs have adapted to every need and whim of their human masters. Humans have selectively bred dogs to alter physical attributes like size, color, leg length, mass and skull diameter in order to suit our own needs and fancies. Dogs serve humans not only as companions and guardians but also as hunters, exterminators, shepherds, rescuers, messengers, warriors, babysitters and more!

Here's a Best in Show Brace from Innisfree: Am/Can. Ch. Innisfree's Red October (male) and Ch. Innisfree's Ginga Hokusa (female).

on November 23, 1949 at Ueno Ikenohata Park and attracted 240 dogs. In 1950, the first issue of the AJGDA's gazette

was published; in 1957 the gazette was renamed *The Companion Dog.*

A second Japanese organization, known as the Japan Dog Federation, was established in 1963 and became an associate member of FCI, the first such gesture toward Japan's interest in the international dog scene. Around this time, the first international judges from the UK and US were invited to judge at Japanese dog shows. By 1971, the newly formed the Asia Kennel Union, established to promote quality pure-breds in the Asian dog world, accepted Japan as its chair. In 1976, the AJGDA became known as the Japan Kennel Club (JKC), and Toyosaku Kariyabu, the third president of the organization, initiated major changes to modernize the organization. In 1982, the first FCI World Dog Show ever to be held in Japan took place in Tokyo. In 1992, the JKC established mutual recognition with the American Kennel Club and Canadian Kennel Club.

According to JKC statistics, the Shiba ranks number 11 in the nation's breed registrations, though Japan's most popular breed is the Dachshund! By the end of the 20th century, the Shiba Inu accounted for about 80% of Nippo's total registrations and, due to its convenient

condo-size, is one of Japan's most popular breeds. Pure-bred dog registrations have skyrocketed in Japan: in 1992 there were over 300,000 dogs registered and 10 years later in 2002 there were over 520,000.

MODERN SHIBA HISTORY

We can trace our modern Shiba to less than a dozen influential ancestors, which were first identified by breeder and Japanese dog scholar, Mr. Ishikawa, who studied the pedigrees of winning dogs to determine which foundation Shibas have had the most lasting influence. Among the two most important were Aka of Fugoku and Naka of Akaishiso. Aka of Fugoku, a red male, passed on his good bone, dense coat, proper angulation and ideal temperament to over 200 litters. Naka of Akaishiso lived in Nagano Prefecture and has been called the father of the Shiba restoration because of his many excellent offspring found throughout Japan.

SHIBAS COME TO AMERICA

Although the Akita made its way to the US in the 1950s, the Shiba did not whistle "Yankee Doodle" until the early 1970s. Some records show that a stray Shiba or two found their way to the US after World War II, but none of these dogs contributed to the establishment of the breed on American soil. The first show in which the Shiba was exhibited was a rare breed show in California, judged by

Toby for short, here's Best in Specialty Show Am/Can. Ch. Innisfree's Red October, owned by the Kanzlers.

In the UK and around the world, the Japanese Shiba has become a consistent winner at shows due to the breed's elegant appearance, sparkling personality and natural beauty.

The first American-bred Shiba Inu to win a rare-breed all-breed Best in Show was Ch. Katuranishiki of Oikawa House, owned by Richard Tomita.

visiting Japanese breeder Mr. Kaiji Katsumoto. The first national specialty of the Shiba Club of America (SCA) took place in October 1981, with Mr. Keiche Jige as judge. The SCA followed the Nippo standard and encouraged others to do so. As is the case with most new breeds, dissension and disagreement reigned supreme and a new club on the east coast was founded, the National Shiba Club of America (NSCA) in 1983. The new club's goal was to seek acceptance by the American Kennel Club (AKC), a goal that the SCA did not embrace. The NSCA was attempting to follow in the steps of the Akita Club of America, which as history would tell us would be a foolhardy path at best! (Consider

the problems of the current Japanese versus American Akita situation, where the American Akita is now called the Great Japanese Dog at FCI shows). Nevertheless, by 1991, the AKC accepted the Shiba into its Miscellaneous Class and into the Non-Sporting Group by June 1993. The first AKC-sanctioned specialty show of the National Shiba Club of America took place in 1993, and Toyojiro of Nidai Maneiso was selected Best of Breed.

Although it is believed that the first Shiba in the US arrived in the mid 1950s, not until the 1970s did imports begin flowing. In the mid 1970s a male dog named Nidai Akajishi of Sagami Ikeda Kensha and a female named Tenshome were imported into the US by Japanese-Americans Kaiji and Toshiko Katsumoto. Although Tenshome had 4 litters, producing 11 puppies, none of the progeny figured into the breed's history, as all were sold as pets. In 1980 Kuromatsume of Sagami Ikeda Kensha, the daughter of Kuroichi of Rozanso, an important Japanese sire, entered the Katsumotos' lives. She was bred to Nidai Akajishi and produced two influential dogs, a male named Shishi of Kenwaso and a female named Shishihime of Kenwaso, both reds.

In 1978 Julia Cadwell, another of the earliest Shiba breeders, imported Shina no Ichihime of Shinshu Mitamuraso, a female whom she bred to a red male that she rescued named Rusty. This litter of four puppies was the official start of her Shosha Shibas kennel. Over the next few years, Cadwell not only imported five excellent Shibas from Japan to establish her own kennel but also brought in Shibas for other American breeders.

Assisted by Cadwell were Frank and Merry Atkinson of the Golden Sun Akitas, who imported a number of Shibas from Japanese

kennels, including the Best of Breed winner of the first and second Shiba Club of America specialties Kuroyuki of Nanko Suzuki Kensha, sired by Kuroichi

Famous American sire, Ryutaro of Yamazakisow Kensha, owned by Richard Tomita, was a multi-Best of Breed winner and sire to many great Shibas in the early 1990s. One of Ryutaro's many daughters is the author's lovely bitch, Maikohime of Akatani ("Kabuki").

Am/Can. Ch. Innisfree's Tali-mon, winning at the NSCA national specialty, owned by the Kanzlers.

of Rozanso. In the early 1980s the Atkinsons started their Ogon Taiyoso Shiba kennels. Soon came along Sheryl Langan, who based her Langans Brushwood Shibas on the Ogon Taiyoso dogs of the Atkinsons, and Frank and Alice Sakayeda, who imported dogs from Japan. Nancy Baugus and Mary Malone based their kennels on imports from Mr. Sakayeda. Seitenhime of Aunso (known as Satori's Mama), imported by Mr. Sakayeda, became the foundation of Ms. Malone's Minimeadow kennels.

Like the Atkinsons, Jean Uchida and Joan Young came to Shibas as experienced Akita people. Young's first two Shibas were bred by Uchida, and these dogs became the basis of her kennel.

In the mid-1980s, world-respected Boxer breeder Richard Tomita, of Jacquet Boxers, imported 15 Shibas from Japan, with the help of Dr. Nakazawa, a vet and show judge. Five of these excellent dogs were from the Oikawa House kennel, including the famous Ch. Katsuranishiki of Oikawa House, known to all on the East coast as "Chibi." Chibi was a top sire and Best in Show-winning dog, not the least of his progeny being the author's beloved house dog, Jacquet's Tengu, whom Tomita has called an improvement on his father.

Progeny of Chibi have the prized feature of improving with age, and Tengu at 13 years of age is still going strong. Mr. Tomita's Shiba program was continued by his sister Christine Tomita-Eicher and handler Don Robinder.

Other breeders came along in the mid 1980s, when the Shiba began to be noticed not only in rare-breed show rings but also by the general public, who became enchanted with this darling Japanese pure-bred. Ed and Terry Arndt (Jade-Shogun) actively promoted and showed the breed in Arizona. Chris Ross of Nevada imported stock from Japan to establish his kennel. Janice Cowen based her program on the Katsumotos' imports as well as dogs from Maran Atha and Gento. Cowen's dogs then contributed to the Foxtrot kennel of Bruce and Kathleen Truax, which became a prominent presence in the breed. The Justa kennels of Jane Chalfant also became active in the mid 1980s and has been influential around the country.

Kathleen and Norbert Kanzler (Innisfree), Tim and Gretchen Haskett (Foxfire), Leslie Ann Engen and Marianne Nixon (San Jo) and Laura Payton (Fanfair) came along in the 1990s and continue to be active in the current-day Shiba scene in the US.

British fanciers continue to embrace the Japanese Shiba. The success of their breeding programs is evidenced by this handsome line-up of show dogs.

SHIBAS IN THE UK

Hailing from the US, not Japan, the first Shibas were sent by Ed and Terry Arndt of Jade-Shogun kennels, Arizona, to the UK in 1985. These three Shibas arrived at Kiskas Akita kennels, owned by Gerald and Kath Mitchell. Among the three dogs was Shogun Hisui Megami, the foundation bitch for Brian and Kath Hindley's Yorlands kennel, an established Rottweiler kennel. The other two Shibas were Shogun Hisui Yukita-mahime (Dixie) and Shogun Hisue Yukihikari (Yen), who would produce the second litter on British soil in October 1986. The three original imported Shibas began their campaign in Britain upon being released from quarantine, starting with a promotional program for Crufts in February 1986. The Hindleys later imported Ogan No Takame Ogon Taiyo So of Kiskas, who was carrying a litter sired by Beni Washi-go. She whelped two pups in quarantine.

The honor of "first litter produced in England" goes to Shogun Hisui Tukihikari Kiskas and Shogun Hisui Megami of Yorlands, who produced two pups on September 7, 1986. The breeder was Kath Hindley. Maureen Atchinson acquired one of Dixie and Yen's pups for her Madason kennel and later imported the first Japanese-born male into the UK, again from the Arndts in the US. He was called Taka for short (his formal name was Tamawakamaru of Madason) and was bred by Mr. Yaichiro Watatsu of Japan.

Only red Shibas had been imported into England thus far, but that was rectified by a few imports. The first red sesame dog to be imported into the UK was a bitch named Camboalijo Ujahime, called Suki. She was owned by John and Dana Ogilvie. The first black and tan was Minimeadows Summer Dream, imported by Joe and Betty Neath. Although these dogs and others were imported, the reds continue to predominate on the British Shiba scene.

Once the Shiba was accepted into the Utility Group,

it began turning heads of fanciers and judges alike. The first Shiba to win a Group and Best in Show was Wellshim Blackjack Is Vormund, who did so in 1991. Challenge Certificates were not offered until 1996, when the first champions were made up. The first Shiba champion was the male Kerrilands Total Majic, bred by Bill and Jenny Cowland, and the first bitch champion was Vormund I'm Smartie, bred by Liz Dunhill.

Established in 1987, the Japanese Shiba Inu Club of Great Britain has been promoting the Shiba steadily

since its inception. Its fortune has been the devoted interest of experienced dog breeders and judges, who have led the way for the Shiba in Britain.

WORLD DOMINATION

The Shiba has begun its campaign of "world domination" and fanciers around the globe unite in their admiration for this Nipponese treasure chest! Down Under breeder, judge and author Arthur Lane was cast under the Shiba's spell in the mid 1970s and since has founded a successful Shiba kennel in Australia.

Many Shibas have been imported from Japan and the UK to establish bloodlines in Australia.

The first Shibas on continental Europe entered Sweden in 1972. Credit is given to the Manloten kennels of Mr. and Mrs. Carolsson. European neighbors soon followed, and imports from England, Japan and the US went to Holland, Denmark, France, Italy and Norway. At most FCI shows on the Continent, a strong Shiba entry is present to represent the breed.

This class of Shibas is competing at the famous Crufts Dog Show in Birmingham, England.

Dancing on her twos, Kabuki is quite an entertaining Shiba. The Shiba Inu's balance and agility, like the breed's spirit and good nature, are impressive.

CHARACTERISTICS OF THE

SHIBA INU

The essence of the Japanese Shiba is quite ineffable... like translating an ancient haiku into English... or describing the knowing glint in your Shiba's deep brown eyes. In the Shiba Inu, there is a purity, a nobility, an essence that is remarkably perfect, remarkably Japanese. Like a tiny sculpture or painting rendered by a skilled Asian craftsman, like an impeccably pruned bonsai tree cultivated by a Japanese gardener, so too is the miniature Japanese wonder we call Shiba Inu.

That the Shiba is a pure-bred dog of ancient lineage cannot be challenged. When an uninformed onlooker first eyes the Shiba, it is clear to even him that this is a special and wondrous canine. By definition, the Shiba is "small" and "well balanced." Balance and harmony, in all great art as in Japanese dogs, are absolute essentials, and the Shiba must be properly proportioned, in head and in expression, in body and in spirit.

The Japanese describe the Shiba's essence with some very interesting words that are difficult to translate, particularly for the Westerner who does not know the Shiba. *Kan-i* means "spirited boldness," a phrase that has been incorporated in the American standard to describe the temperament of the Shiba—"brave, bold, alert, calm and controlled." The Japanese word *ryosei* translates as "good-natured," also used in the standard, as the Shiba is first and foremost a companion dog. *Soboku* refers to the Shiba's gentleness and modesty, both qualities that underlie the breed's natural sense of dignity.

The breed standard, which is a written description of the ideal representative of the breed, is eye-opening indeed regarding the character of the Shiba. The American standard suits the author's needs more so than the English standard, which defines characteristics as "bright, active, keen and alert, also docile and faithful." (Unfortunately the English Kennel Club standard could be describing any breed of dog, mongrel, or perhaps even a cat or rabbit.) The AKC standard adeptly defines the Shiba's temperament: "A spirited boldness, a good nature, and an unaffected forthrightness, which together yield dignity and natural beauty. The Shiba has an independent nature and can be reserved toward strangers but is loyal and affectionate to those who earn his respect. At times aggressive toward other dogs, the Shiba is always under the control of his handler."

"Unaffected forthrightness" strikes a resonant chord with the Shiba owner. The breed's nobility and dignity are as natural as his primitive dog behavior. There is nothing affected or superficial about the Shiba's character. The breed is natural in both spirit and physique. Nothing is exaggerated about the Shiba's canine structure, which is comparable to that of the wolf or fox—natural—or perhaps a wild dog like the Australian dingo, an animal that appears Shiba-like in some respects but lacks the refinement and subtle balance of the Japanese dog.

ARE YOU A SHIBA PERSON?
Having lived with Shibas for nearly 15 years, this author feels as qualified as any to recommend the Shiba to the right owner. You could not find a more delightful, life-loving, appealing dog anywhere in the world. Shibas, by and large, are healthy and long-lived and relatively undemanding of their owners. Their size is perfect: not so small that they can be misplaced and sat upon, as could a toy breed, and not so large that an owner can't whisk them into his arms and be on his

The author wholeheartedly recommends the Shiba to the right person. These are delightful, energetic and intelligent dogs that demand commitment and patience from their owners...on an hourly basis!

way. Temperamentally, Shibas are trustworthy and loyal, alert, charismatic and intelligent. Shibas are clean, resourceful and great fun for children.

However, no breed of dog is for everyone, and the Shiba is no exception. The Shiba is an independent dog that has a mind that rivals that of the smartest owner. Training a Shiba is a test of wills, and Shibas despise repetition. These are intense and serious dogs that can find a way to solve any problem. Yet, in true Japanese style, Shibas are as stubborn as they are independent and smart. Shibas can concentrate on a problem for hours and then work a way out of the dilemma. (Can Shibas think?—don't let them hear you say that!) A Shiba's training (teaching session, please!) must begin as early as six to eight weeks. For other breeds, this may be too young, but the Shiba will start to work things out before you do and then convince you that you are doing them wrong. Case in point, leash training! Don't wait or you will have a life-long struggle at the other end of the lead.

THE CAT'S MEOW
The quality that originally attracted me to the Shiba was its "cat-like behavior." Like felines, Shibas are very clean and will spend hours grooming themselves. (Shibas know that

they are beauties, just as cats do.) If you live in an apartment on the tenth floor, you can even train your Shiba to use a litter box, though it's not wholeheartedly recommended. Shibas use their paws in cleaning themselves and in playing the same way cats do. My female, Kabuki, even climbs into windowsills to watch over the yard. Shibas' intensity and concentration are as feline as a metaphysical poem. Shibas are also catlike in their love of chasing small animals, such as mice or birds. They are reckless in their pursuit of a furry or feathered foe. I have seen Kabuki leap into the air after a bird on the wing. Also like cats, Shibas are preternaturally smart and therefore are difficult to train.

One last word about cats.

Shibas welcome the company of well-behaved children who don't mind a little affection. Here Alyse Badal receives a wet hello from Kabuki.

HEART-HEALTHY

In this modern age of ever-improving cardio-care, no doctor or scientist can dispute the advantages of owning a dog to lower a person's risk of heart disease. Studies have proven that petting a dog, walking a dog and grooming a dog all show positive results toward lowering your blood pressure. The simple routine of exercising your dog—going outside with the dog and walking, jogging or playing catch—is heart-healthy in and of itself. If you are normally less active than your physician thinks you should be, adopting a dog may be a smart option to improve your own quality of life as well as that of another creature.

Shibas don't particularly like cats, perhaps because they are too much like themselves. With proper introductions and close supervision, an owner can trust a Shiba and a cat. The author's two Shibas live with three Bengal cats....quite willingly. Kabuki rather likes them and will groom them (when the cats permit), though my male, Tengu, defiantly acts as the "Bengal Warden" and will attempt to bully them (especially when they're sleeping!). Tengu is a typical Shiba male, brimming with self-importance.

OPERATION HOUDINI

Shiba owners are forewarned! Keeping Shibas is more difficult than just keeping Shibas! No matter how perfect a home you provide for your Shiba, it is the Shiba's nature to treat a human abode as a prison and his only goal in life is to escape! Freedom is the sweetest reward and every Shiba is devoted to tasting it. It seems as if the "call of the wild" or the allure of the Japanese homeland is so strong in the Shiba that they must run free. Combined with the Shiba's intelligence, craftiness, small size, agility and intensity, this need to escape is a concern for all owners.

I have witnessed adult Shibas in crates at dog shows unhook the locks on their crates just to have a look-see about the show grounds.

Kabuki and one of her Bengal cats, Jazzman, have a very open relationship. Kabuki met Jazzman as a kitten when she was five years old and accepted him as part of the family. Socialization and confident instruction are key in introducing a new pet into one's household.

My own Shibas have found ways to open the front gates to the yard so that they can roam the neighborhood. A fence is no security against the Shiba obsessed with escaping. Shibas are remarkable diggers, able to burrow under a fence with their catlike feet and nails and strong forequarters. While they are small, they are still agile enough to climb a fence, using the paws and teeth to effect the escape!

"SELECTIVE HEARING"

Shibas have keen senses, as they were bred to hunt by sight and smell. Although the Shiba has perfectly normal ears, they don't work as well as an owner might expect. This phenomenon is known as "selective hearing disorder." Shibas choose not to hear their owners when they use certain commands, especially "Come" or "No." (Mysteriously, they can always hear words like "eat," "walk," and "playtime.") For a dog that lives to run away, this selective hearing is a real problem for Shiba owners.

By the grace of God and pure luck, the author has been able to keep both his Shibas for over ten years. One trick that the author has relied on is related to the Shiba's sensitivity to scolding and correction. Shibas are independent but do not like to fail or disappoint. When Kabuki starts to bolt, I immediately hurl reprimands her way (the neighbors love this!). "Bad dog!" "Bad girl!" (be creative here). Fortunately, she is so overwhelmed by my disappointment and scolding that she stops dead in her tracks and rolls over! She waits for me to pick her up and carry her home. In true Shiba fashion, her ears are folded back and she shows just enough of her gums to paint a pathetic portrait.

THE MIGHTY HUNTER

Every book written on the Shiba claims that this is a superb hunting dog, blessed with astute instincts and skill. If the new owner is selecting a Shiba for hunting, he might wish to rethink his strategy. Choosing a Shiba to hunt is akin to choosing an Italian Greyhound to race! We have all read romantic stories of Shibas carrying home 50 quails or 8 dozen hares, but such dogs are rare indeed.

Historically in Japan, the Shiba has been employed by hunters for pheasants and ducks as well as small wild animals, such as rabbits, squirrels and weasels. The Shiba trained to hunt pheasants does not, in fact, retrieve or flush the bird, as would a gundog, but trees the bird, as would a coonhound in pursuit of a raccoon. The hunter is then able to locate the bird from the Shiba's barking and then shoot the pheasant. Japanese hunters have trained Shibas as decoys for duck hunting as well. The Shibas lure the ducks to the shore, intrigued by the Shiba's wagging tail and barking enthusiasm. Shibas are traditionally used for either bird hunting or small-mammal hunting, rarely both. Once the Shiba has a taste for catching a rabbit, it will always be distracted by any twitching in the grass and thereby forget about luring or treeing the birds.

Although Shibas may not get much on-the-field experience today, their chase instincts are surely intact. Most Shibas will pursue and catch small mammals with little to no effort, particularly rodents and rabbits. The Shiba's nose is extremely sensitive and able to detect a burrowing rodent with the precision of a terrier. Swift and animated, the Shiba can outrun a rabbit and kill it with grace and dexterity. While most Shiba owners don't relish such gifts from their dogs, it is not uncommon for the Shiba to deliver a rat or a rabbit to his owner's feet—and always with that unmistakable Shiba smile!

KABUKI THEATRICS

Japan has two original theatrical forms, the Kabuki theater and the Nōh theater. The former is known for its highly ritualistic

DELTA SOCIETY

The human-animal bond propels the work of the Delta Society, striving to improve the lives of people and animals. The Pet Partners Program proves that the lives of people and dogs are inextricably linked. The Pet Partners Program, a national registry, trains and screens volunteers for pet therapy in hospices, nursing homes, schools and rehabilitation centers. Dog-and-handler teams of Pet Partners volunteer in all 50 states, with nearly 7,000 teams making visits annually. About 900,000 patients, residents and students receive assistance each year. If you and your dog are interested in becoming Pet Partners, contact the Delta Society online at www.deltasociety.org.

movement and exaggerated vocal style and the latter is known for its more subtle classical pageantry. Without a doubt, the Shiba subscribes to the Kabuki approach to life (and doesn't even recognize the word "Nōh."). The author's bitch was thus named Kabuki because of her broad theatrical mannerisms, even though for her first year she probably thought her name was "Nōh." Like a true Shiba, she dances on her hind feet to express her delight; she screams, screeches and squeaks to vocalize her dismay and her discontent; she jumps, leaps, twists and rolls to convey her various moods and desires. There is nothing subtle about Kabuki.

Shibas are very expressive with their voices and are capable of making many unusual canine sounds, including monkey-like squealing, parrot-like honking and earth-shattering screams. Despite this impressive vocabulary, Shibas are not necessarily vocal dogs and use their barks most discreetly. For some Shibas, barking is a last resort (when the more interesting squeaking and squawking fail to get the desired response). Shibas will bark when a stranger approaches the front door, though they will not bark for the sake of barking and have no interest in repeating such a mundane utterance.

MALE VS. FEMALE

There are positive and negative aspects of both sexes when selecting a Shiba. The female is naturally maternal, making a loving and demonstrative companion for both adults and children. Females are easier to house-train, though lead training is not necessarily any easier. Males tend to be more stubborn, especially where matters of the bladder are concerned. Both male and female Shibas are territorial, though females tend to be more aggressive than males. Bitches are more likely to engage in a fight than are males, which is not necessarily so with most other breeds. Two bitches will fight as sure as the Japanese sun will rise! Females tend to be more straightforward with their emotions while males seem more reserved, though once the love of a male Shiba is earned, it is steadfast and true. Females tend to be more flighty and fun-loving. Males may be more adventure-seeking than females, a result of their need to spray the whole neighborhood every day. In general, females are more outgoing and friendly, while males are more reserved with people they don't know. Every Shiba is a unique and wondrous creature, and you may find male Shibas who behave like females and vice-versa. So much for generalization!

HEALTH CONCERNS
FOR SHIBA OWNERS

Compared to many other pure-bred dogs, Shibas are graced with good health and relative freedom from hereditary problems. The most common problem in Shibas is slipped kneecaps, more properly called luxated patellas. This condition can either be hereditary or caused by an accident. As a result of the kneecap slipping out of position, it is weaker from the distress.

More stressful for Shibas are hot spots, which are a form of moist dermatitis that occurs on the Shiba's rear quarters, usually on the back under the tail or on the tail itself. Other locations include the thighs, ears or around the mouth. The dog will bite and scratch the spot until it is raw and irritated. Seek veterinary assistance, as an injection of antihistamine and clipping the affected area will provide relief.

Monorchids and cryptorchids are a concern in every breed, and the Shiba is no exception. These conditions, marked by one or both testicles not descending properly in the scrotum, are cause for disqualification in the show ring and are hereditary. Such animals should be excluded from breeding programs. Male Shibas mature slowly and may require up to ten months for both testicles to descend.

Ear problems are also

common in Shibas, usually caused by mites. Suffering dogs will shake their heads and scratch at their ears. Proper cleaning of the ears and drops prescribed by your vet will alleviate the problem. Shibas hate to have their ears fussed with, so check the ears regularly to be certain that no residue or odor is detectable.

Eye concerns include progressive retinal atrophy, an hereditary condition that can lead to blindness in many breeds, as well as entropion and trichiasis, both of which are disorders of the eye lids and lashes. Breeders should screen for these eye problems in their dogs to keep the Shiba free of such debilitating problems. Concerned breeders register their dogs' eye test results with the Canine Eye Registration Foundation (CERF). Likewise, breeders are screening their Shibas for hip dysplasia and reporting their results to the Orthopedic Foundation for Animals (OFA) or PennHIP.

An informed new owner will recognize a well-bred, healthy litter of Shiba puppies. Discuss breed health with your chosen breeder.

SHIBA INU

A breed standard is a written description of the ideal representative of a breed. This description is used by judges, breeders and exhibitors to guide them in their selection, breeding and promotion of the best dogs. At dog shows, the judges compare each dog entered to the dog described in the breed standard. The Shiba Inu that most closely "conforms" to the standard is selected as the winner. For this reason, dog shows are sometimes called "conformation competitions."

Breed standards are drafted by the parent club (like the National Shiba Club of America or Nippo).

In discussing the Shiba standard, there are four standards of importance: 1. The original Japanese standard (Nippo); 2. The American Kennel Club standard; 3. The Kennel Club standard (the current English standard); 4. The FCI standard (used throughout Europe and beyond). In essence, all four standards describe the same dog, though they vary in wording, content and completeness. Here we present the American Kennel Club standard and then we will discuss differences between it and the others.

AMERICAN KENNEL CLUB STANDARD FOR THE SHIBA INU

GENERAL APPEARANCE

The Shiba is the smallest of the Japanese native breeds of dog and was originally developed for hunting by sight and scent in the dense undergrowth of Japan's mountainous areas. Alert and agile with keen senses, he is also an excellent watchdog and companion. His frame is compact

The Shiba should be a small, well balanced, sturdy dog with a keen and alert temperament.

with well-developed muscles. Males and females are distinctly different in appearance: males are masculine without coarseness, females are feminine without weakness of structure.

The shape, size and color of the eyes contribute to the Shiba's expression, which, to some, is Oriental and feline.

SIZE, PROPORTION, SUBSTANCE
Males 14.5 inches to 16.5 inches at withers. Females 13.5 inches to 15.5 inches. The preferred size is the middle of the range for each sex. Average weight at preferred size is approximately 23 pounds for males, 17 pounds for females. Males have a height to length ratio of 10 to 11, females slightly longer. Bone is moderate. *Disqualification*—Males over 16.5 inches and under 14.5 inches. Females over 15.5 inches and under 13.5 inches.

HEAD
Expression is good natured with a strong and confident gaze. Eyes are somewhat triangular in shape, deep set, and upward slanting toward the outside base of the ear. Iris is dark brown. Eye rims are black. Ears are triangular in shape, firmly pricked and small, but in proportion to head and body size. Ears are set well apart and tilt directly forward with the slant of the back of the ear following the arch of the neck. Skull size is moderate and in proportion to the body. Forehead is broad and flat with a slight furrow. Stop is moderate. Muzzle is firm, full, and round with a stronger lower jaw projecting from full cheeks. The bridge of the muzzle is straight. Muzzle tapers slightly from stop to nose tip. Muzzle length is 40% of the total head length from occiput to nose tip. It is preferred that whiskers remain intact. Lips are tight and black. Nose is black. Bite is scissors, with a full complement of strong, substantial, evenly aligned teeth. *Serious fault:* Five or more missing teeth is a very serious fault and must be penalized. *Disqualification*—Overshot or undershot bite.

NECK, TOPLINE AND BODY
Neck is thick, sturdy, and of moderate length. Topline is straight and level to the base of the tail. Body is dry and well muscled without the appearance

of sluggishness or coarseness. Forechest is well developed. Chest depth measured from the withers to the lowest point of the sternum is one-half or slightly less than the total height from withers to ground. Ribs are moderately sprung. Abdomen is firm and well tucked-up. Back is firm. Loins are strong. Tail is thick and powerful and is carried over the back in a sickle or curled position. A loose single curl or sickle tail pointing vigorously toward the neck and nearly parallel to the back is preferred. A double curl or sickle tail pointing upward is acceptable. In length the tail reaches nearly to the hock joint when extended. Tail is set high.

FOREQUARTERS

Shoulder blade and upper arm are moderately angulated and approximately equal in length. Elbows are set close to the body and turn neither in nor out. Forelegs and feet are moderately spaced,

White markings in red dogs are restricted to eye spots, cheeks, underjaw, forechest, underparts, and underside of tail and legs.

straight, and parallel. Pasterns are slightly inclined. Removal of front dewclaws is optional. Feet are catlike with well-arched toes fitting tightly together. Pads are thick.

HINDQUARTERS

The angulation of the hindquarters is moderate and in balance with the angulation of the forequarters. Hind legs are strong with a wide natural stance. The hock joint is strong, turning neither in nor out. Upper thighs are long and the second thighs short but well developed. No dewclaws. Feet as in forequarters.

COAT

Double coated with the outer coat being stiff and straight and the undercoat soft and thick. Fur is short and even on face, ears, and legs. Guard hairs stand off the body are about 1.5 to 2 inches in length at the withers. Tail hair is slightly longer and stands open in a brush. It is preferred that the Shiba be presented in a natural state. Trimming of the coat must be severely penalized. *Serious fault*—Long or woolly coat.

COLOR

Coat color is as specified herein, with the three allowed colors given equal consideration. All colors are clear and intense. The undercoat is cream, buff or gray. *Urajiro* (cream to white ventral color) is required in the following areas on all coat colors: on the sides of the muzzle, on the cheeks, inside the ears, on the underjaw and upper throat, inside of legs, on the abdomen, around the vent and the ventral side of the tail. On reds: commonly on the throat, forechest, and chest. On blacks and sesames: commonly as a triangular mark on both sides of the forechest. White spots above the eyes permitted on all colors but not required.

Bright orange-red with urajiro lending a foxlike appearance to dogs of this color. Clear red preferred but a very slight dash of black tipping is permitted on the back and tail.

Black with tan points and urajiro. Black hairs have a brownish cast, not blue. The undercoat is buff or gray. The borderline between black and tan areas is clearly defined. Tan points are located as follows: two oval spots over the eyes; on the sides of the muzzle between the black bridge of the muzzle and the white cheeks; on the outside of the forelegs from the carpus, or a little above, downward to the toes; on the outside of the hind legs down the front of the stifle broadening from hock joint to toes, but not completely eliminating black from rear of pasterns. Black penciling on toes permitted. Tan hairs may also be found on the inside of the ear and on the underside of the tail. *Sesame* (black-tipped hairs on a rich red background) with urajiro. Tipping is light and even on the body and head with no concentration of black in any area. Sesame areas appear at least one-half red. Sesame may end in a widow's peak on the forehead, leaving the bridge and sides of the muzzle red. Eye spots and lower legs are also red.

Clearly delineated white markings are permitted but not required on the tip of the tail and in the form of socks on the forelegs to the elbow joint, hind legs to the knee joint. A patch of blaze is permitted on the throat, forechest, or chest in addition to urajiro.

Serious fault—Cream, white pinto, or any other color or marking not specified is a very serious fault and must be penalized.

GAIT
Movement is nimble, light, and elastic. At the trot, the legs angle in towards a center line while the topline remains level and firm. Forward reach and rear extension are moderate and efficient. In the show ring, the Shiba is gaited on a loose lead at a brisk trot.

TEMPERAMENT
A spirited boldness, a good nature, and an unaffected forthrightness, which together

The judge uses the mental picture conjured by the breed standard when he accesses each Shiba entered in competition. Dog shows revolve around the judge's interpretation of the written standard.

yield dignity and natural beauty. The Shiba has an independent nature and can be reserved toward strangers but is loyal and affectionate to those who earn his respect. At times aggressive toward other dogs, the Shiba is always under the control of his handler. Any aggression toward handler or judge or any overt shyness must be severely penalized.

The correct Shiba head has a black nose, tight lips and a straight muzzle of good depth. The bitch has a decidedly feminine appeal.

SUMMARY

The foregoing is a description of the ideal Shiba. Any deviation from the above standard is to be considered a fault and must be penalized. The severity of the fault is equal to the extent of the deviation. A harmonious balance of form, color, movement, and temperament is more critical than any one feature.

DISQUALIFICATIONS

Males over 16.5 and under 14.5 inches. Females over 15.5 and under 13.5 inches. Overshot or undershot bite.

Approved February 7, 1997
Effective March 31, 1997

DISCUSSION AND COMPARISON OF THE BREED STANDARDS

The British standard describes the General Appearance of the Shiba similarly but states that the body is "very slightly longer than height at withers." It is the AKC standard that emphasizes the differences between the sexes, stating, "Males and females are distinctly different in appearance: males are masculine without coarseness, females are feminine without weakness of structure." The original Nippo standard supports this notion, recognizing that refined species should show apparent differences in the sexes: "Males and females are obviously distinct, with proportioned bodies." Males are more vigorous, stocky and muscular, always moving with confidence. The male's head is wide and flat, slightly longer than the female's head, which is finer and slightly narrower.

The FCI standard adds: "Constitution strong. Action quick, free and beautiful" as well as a section on "Utilization" that reads "Hunting dog for birds and small animals. Companion dog."

Regarding the description of the Shiba's temperament, the American standard paints a concise portrait: "A spirited boldness, a good nature and an unaffected forthrightness, which together yield dignity and natural beauty." The standard continues to describe the breed's independence and aloofness with strangers. The early (1935) Nippo standard describes the breed's nature and expression quite differently: "Sharp and fierce with good natured simplicity and excellent scenting powers. The whole behavior shows liveliness." Similarly, the current Nippo standard states: "The dog has a spirited boldness with a good nature and a feeling of artlessness. It is alert and able to move quickly with nimble, elastic steps."

The Shiba is considered to be a "head breed," meaning that the correct head is crucial to correct type. In profile, the forehead appears flat and broad, "wide," according to the Nippo standard. The English standard describes the head as like a blunt triangle when viewed from above. The cheeks are very full and "well developed." The stop is moderate in profile, with a hardly visible furrow. The

English standard does not fully concur, stating, "Definite stop with slight furrow." The Shiba's muzzle is firm, thick, full and round, projecting from the full cheeks.

The shape and color of the eyes also contribute to the correct Shiba Inu expression. Described as somewhat triangular in shape, deep set, and upward slanting toward the outside base of the ear, the eyes give the breed its distinctive Asian flair. The Shiba's eyes are small, though in the female's more refined head they may appear slightly larger than those of the male. The eyes are the windows to the Shiba's soul, and his gaze conveys intelligence, worldliness and confidence.

The placement, size and shape of the Shiba's ears also affect expression and correct balance. The ears are small and well furred, creating a desirable hooded effect. The placement and carriage of the ears profoundly affect the breed's correct expression, and the AKC standard describes them appropriately: "set well apart and tilt directly forward with the slant of the back of the ear following the arch of the neck." The Nippo standard indicates some common Shiba ear faults that are believed to be inherent in certain lines and to be avoided: "Thin ear leather, ears that are narrow at the bottom, high ear-set, long ears, flapping of the ear tip, incorrect ear lines, and lack of forward slant." The desired triangular shape should have two equal sides (isosceles), each side extending slightly down the side of the Shiba's head.

Teeth have always been a "sore point" in the Shiba standard, as the breed is notorious for missing teeth. The Nippo standard indicates that "A Shiba with more than four minus marks will not be ranked." The standard sets up deductions for each missing tooth: First premolars equal one minus mark; second premolars equal three minus marks; any other missing tooth equals five minus marks. Judges must concentrate on awarding Shibas with full dentitions—42 teeth, to be exact. By and large, the Shiba mouth is strong and sturdy with sizeable teeth, unlike many toy breeds that suffer similar problems. Ignoring the need for a full dentition can only do harm to the breed.

The neck is well developed and in males appears more well-muscled than the female's refined neck. The neck is crucial to the harmony of the Shiba's outline. The body, according to the AKC standard,

The red Shiba has become the most popular color and far outnumbers the red sesames and black and tans.

"is dry and well muscled without the appearance of sluggishness or coarseness." The Shiba's chest is well developed and powerful; it appears to be the center of the body, contrasting with the well-tucked belly. Both the AKC and Nippo standards state that the Shiba's topline is straight. Angulation is key to the overall balance of the dog. The FCI standard states: "Forequarters: Shoulders moderately sloping, elbows tight; seen from the front, forelegs straight." The hindquarters are described thus: "Upper thighs long, lower thighs short, but well developed. Hocks thick and tough." Breeders consider a 30-

A lovely red Shiba's head, showing exquisite expression, a well-padded muzzle, small, well-furred ears and white marks over the eyes, on the cheeks and on the neck and chest.

compared to "fur" or a "pelt" while the latter style has a more resilient uniform quality. Note also that the Shiba's coat is not a long coat, but rather medium in length. Just as in Akitas, longcoat puppies do occur. These dogs make fine pets, requiring a little extra grooming, though they should not be bred or exhibited.

Colors in Shibas have also been debated in breed circles. Although the British Kennel Club standard still permits four colors to be exhibited, the Japanese and American standards permit only three colors. The English standard permits white dogs (with red or gray tinges) even though the Nippo standard states that white coat color is not desirable. In Japanese dogs, white can be seen on breeds other than the Shiba, including the Kishu (which is usually white) as well as the Akita. In respect to the Japanese homeland of the Shiba Inu, the white coloration should not be promoted in the UK or elsewhere. The interim Kennel Club standard referred also to brindles and grays being accept-able in Shibas—these fortunately do not exist, so the issue passed without debate.

The American Kennel Club, FCI and Nippo use a term in their standards to describe the

degree layback of the shoulders ideal for the Shiba when moving. The rear legs must be strong and flexible, the driving force for Shiba locomotion. Over-angulated stifles are a detriment to proper Shiba gait, as is too wide or narrow a stance.

The Shiba's coat is typical of the spitz dogs, a hard outer coat and a soft undercoat. Depending on the dog's heritage, the Shiba coat can appear full with a generous undercoat and straight guard hairs or thick and dense, appearing somewhat flatter. The former style coat can be

cream to white ventral colors—
urajiro. These markings are
required on all coat colors as
follows: "on the sides of the
muzzle, and on the cheeks, on
the underside of the jaw and
neck, on the chest and stomach
and the underside of the tail,
and on the inside of the legs."
(FCI).

Gait in the Shiba is equivalent to the dog's whole being.
The standards all seem to agree
about how the breed appears on
the move: "Light, quick and
energetic," as the English
standard testifies.

The Shiba tail, last but not
least, is a hallmark of the breed,
held in curl or curved in a
sickle. It should be thickly
furred and (when straightened
out) reach nearly to the hock
joint. Along with the head, the
correct tail balances the overall
Shiba picture. The tail is strong
and expressive, essential for the
breed's quick movement and
balance. The hair on the tail is
longer than anywhere else on
the body.

The FCI standard includes
the following faults: shyness,
bitchy dogs, doggy bitches,
malocclusion (overshot or
undershot mouth), and
numerous missing teeth. The
FCI disqualifications include:
ears not pricked and hanging or
short tail. The AKC standard
disqualifies overshot or

The standard
requires that the
forechest is well
developed and the
forelegs straight
and parallel.

undershot bites as well as males
over 16.5 in and under 14.5 in
and females over 15.5 in and
under 13.5 in. The Nippo
standard faults developmental
defects and nutritional
deficiency, disharmony between
the color of the body and the
color of the nose, white spots in
colored areas of the coat and
short tail caused by genetic
defect. Nippo disqualifies any
dog lacking the quality of a
Japanese dog and any dog with
an overshot or undershot bite.

SHIBA INU

THE INTERROGATION

So you perceive yourself as Shiba Inu material? You feel worthy of owning one of the Shiba breed, but…how well do you satisfy the Shiba's expectations? Please consider the following:

1. How much time do you have to devote to a Shiba each day? Do you work all day? Is your evening schedule bustling with social activities?

2. What kind of home can you provide for your Shiba? Although Shibas do quite well in cities, apartments that are too small may be too confining for the Shiba.

3. Do you have a yard in which the Shiba can run and play? Is the yard *securely* fenced?

4. Do all members of the family welcome the arrival of this energetic ball of spitz fur?

5. Do you have allergies? Shibas cast their coat twice a year and may aggravate an existing allergy.

6. Are you a cleaning fanatic? Shibas are tidy, but they do cover their surroundings with fur at least twice a year. Bitches in season may blow coat an additional time as well.

7. Are you fit and lively? Keeping up with a Shiba on the other end of a lead requires considerable physical fitness. Chasing a Shiba requires even more! Shibas are always on the go—ready to explore and ready to run. Are you physically up to the Shiba challenge?

8. Do you have the time and patience required by the grooming and training of a Shiba puppy? Shibas learn very fast—when they want to. They can be very stubborn. Grooming chores are not too time-consuming, though a weekly session is advisable. Baths are the real chore, as most Shibas don't welcome time in the bath.

PET INSURANCE

Just as you can insure your car, your house and your own health, you likewise can insure your dog's health. Investigate a pet insurance policy by talking to your vet. Depending on the age of your dog, the breed and the kind of coverage you desire, your policy can be very affordable. Most policies cover accidental injuries, poisoning and thousands of medical problems and illnesses, including cancers. Some carriers also offer routine care and immunization coverage.

9. Do you have children in the family? While Shibas are reasonably fond of children (depending on their behavior), they are still quite small dogs and will only tolerate a limited amount of rough play and mishandling.

10. Do you plan frequent vacations? Shibas prefer to be home or with their owners. Boarding a Shiba frequently will be stressful to the dog.

11. Are you willing to devote 12 to 14 years to the life of your Shiba? Thankfully, the Shiba Inu is

Breeder Richard Tomita with a young Shiba pup ready for a new pet home. Find a breeder who cares for his dogs and is willing to make you a part of his extended "dog family."

a long-lived little dog that remains active for most of its years.

12. Do you have the financial ability to provide your Shiba with proper veterinary care, food and upkeep for the whole of his life?

FINDING A SHIBA BREEDER

If you have passed this test, then you are ready to consider how to go about locating a Shiba puppy. Admittedly it is difficult for the potential owner to contain his excitement about adopting a Shiba pup. Few breeds have the "puppy appeal" of the Shiba...with their plush cuteness, tiny ears, dark eyes and curvy tail...plus the Shiba puppy swish...racing around the floor or trying to mount steps. The author implores new owners to do their homework before venturing into ownership. New owners must find the right

---

FINDING A QUALIFIED BREEDER

Before you begin your puppy search, ask for references from your veterinarian and perhaps other breeders to refer you to someone they believe is reputable. Responsible breeders usually raise only one or two breeds of dog. Avoid any breeder who has several different breeds or has several litters at the same time. Dedicated breeders are usually involved with a breed or other dog club. Many participate in some sport or activity related to their breed. Just as you want to be assured of the breeder's qualifications, the breeder wants to be assured that you will make a worthy owner. Expect the breeder to interview you, asking questions about your goals for the pup, your experience with dogs and what kind of home you will provide.

PEDIGREE VS. REGISTRATION CERTIFICATE

Too often new owners are confused between these two important documents. Your puppy's pedigree, essentially a family tree, is a written record of a dog's genealogy of three generations or more. The pedigree will show you the names as well as performance titles of all dogs in your pup's background. Your breeder must provide you with a registration application, with his part properly filled out. You must complete the application and send it to the AKC with the proper fee. Every puppy must come from a litter that has been AKC-registered by the breeder, born in the USA and from a sire and dam that are also registered with the AKC.

The seller must provide you with complete records to identify the puppy. The AKC requires that the seller provide the buyer with the following: breed; sex, color and markings; date of birth; litter number (when available); names and registration numbers of the parents; breeder's name; and date sold or delivered.

good Shiba breeder has likely been "in the breed" for a decade or more and has seen four or five generations of his line. The best source for a Shiba breeder directory is the National Shiba Club of America. Visit them online at www.shibas.org. For the owner who is serious about acquiring a top-quality potentially showable Shiba, a visit to a dog show and a perusal of the catalog is time well spent. The dogs in the catalog are listed by their full AKC names, which usually include a kennel prefix (such as Innisfree, Akemi, Koma-Inu and Frerose). Finding the quality breeders attached to these kennels is an obvious first step. Foundation breeders like Julia Cadwell, Frank and Merry Atkinson, Frank and Alice Sakayeda and Kathleen Kanzler have established "Shiba families," fanciers who have their bloodlines and expand to create "sublines."

Even though the Shiba Inu is considered a hot new breed in the US, especially in the urban centers, it is still possible to meet "the right people" in the breed to get started. If you approach owners at a dog show when they are not busy grooming or handling the dogs, most Shiba fanciers are willing to talk to you about their favorite topic: Shibas! These folk are ideal for recommending breeders who are

breeder and the right puppy. Shiba breeders in the US are a growing clan, though there aren't too many breeders who have as many years' experience as the German Shepherd or Collie breeders whom a new owner might encounter in looking for those more popular breeds. A expecting a litter and teaching you the ins and outs of the Shiba world. You may also contact the American Kennel Club for a list of qualified Shiba breeders in your area.

There is a tremendous difference between buying a puppy and purchasing a car or a bedroom set. Breeders are not salespeople. They are not looking to "unload" a puppy on any anxious buyer who has the money. You will not get a discount, and in the dog world you get what you pay for! Expect the breeder to ask you many questions about your intentions, experience with dog ownership, time constraints, accommodations, etc. The questions at the beginning of this chapter will be on the breeder's list as well.

Good breeders do not feel that you are their customers; they feel that you are adopting one of their children. Since Shibas have relatively small litters (from two to six puppies), selection at a kennel will not be great. Breeders often retain a puppy for show purposes and have a waiting list of potential owners who have passed their interview process. Be wary of the breeder who asks no questions and sells you a pup on the spot without any hesitation.

Owners should always inquire of the breeder about health screening, problems in their lines, including behavioral,

and ask to meet the sire and dam (and possible other relatives) of the puppy. Consider how the breeder relates to his dogs. Is he familiar with all of them? Do the dogs crave his attention? Is there obvious admiration in the dogs' eyes when they look at the breeder? These are all subtle signs that the breeder is a responsible, caring individual who wants to see his progeny go to proper

NEW RELEASES

Most breeders release their puppies between seven and ten weeks of age. A breeder who allows puppies to leave the litter at five or six weeks of age may be more concerned with profit than with the puppies' welfare. However, some breeders of show or working breeds may hold one or more top-quality puppies longer, occasionally until three or four months of age, in order to evaluate the puppies' career or show potential and decide which one(s) they will keep for themselves.

A SHOW PUPPY

If you plan to show your puppy, you must first deal with a reputable breeder who shows his dogs and has had some success in the conformation ring. The puppy's pedigree should include one or more champions in the first and second generation. You should be familiar with the breed and breed standard so you can know what qualities to look for in your puppy. The breeder's observations and recommendations also are invaluable aids in selecting your future champion. If you consider an older puppy, be sure that the puppy has been properly socialized with people and not isolated in a kennel without substantial daily human contact.

homes where they will stay for their whole lives. Responsible breeders will also take back any puppy that an owner decides is

not right for his lifestyle. Dog breeders rarely care about the money, as the dogs and the breed come first. By the same token, this doesn't mean that you should not pay top price for your puppy. The breeder's program is very costly, and it's necessary that owners pay full price for every puppy in the litter in order for the kennel to remain operational.

SELECTING A SHIBA PUPPY

Shiba puppies are irresistible, no matter what kind of dog you prefer. Shibas look like tiny fox pups with their jet black noses and deep brown eyes. If you view the litter at about three or four weeks of age, the colors of the puppies will be quite similar. Red and red sesame puppies will show a good deal of black hair, which lightens in reds as the undercoat grows in. All Shibas have black masks that fade as the puppy develops. The tiny ears take a few weeks to become erect and will be well furred by the fifth or sixth week. The pigment on the pup's nose, eye lids, paw pads and lips should be jet black. Even as a puppy, the Shiba has a blunt triangular head shape and a well-padded muzzle. White markings (urajiro) begin to emerge between the fifth and sixth week on the Shiba's face, underparts and chest. Be sure that the Shiba puppy's bite is neither undershot or overshot. It's not prudent to count teeth on a six-week-old puppy, but you may ask the breeder to show you the parents' bites if you are serious about showing your puppy.

The six-week-old puppy should radiate its Shiba spirit. These tiny puppies know that they are a "chosen race" and glow with confidence and that celebrated sense of self-importance that Shiba fanciers adore. The litter should be energetic and happy-go-lucky, ready to overwhelm visitors with their antics. Not all Shiba puppies do act the same. There may be a more reserved puppy in the litter, less inclined to greet visitors but nonetheless interested in his surroundings. Do not mistake this pup for a shy or "spooky" puppy. This pup has a typical Shiba Inu intellect, reserved in the usual "Oriental" fashion. Shiba puppies by and large should look like miniature versions of adults and do not change too dramatically as they grow. As the breed is such a natural canine, its development is quite predictable.

Rely on your breeder to recommend which Shiba puppy is suited to your lifestyle. Shibas have unique personalities that emerge early on, and the breeder will know which pup will be the clown, the intellect, the wanderer, the lover, etc. No matter what the personality of the Shiba puppy, all pups can make a smiling,

loving addition to the right home. Shibas promise to perk up any household, and owners must be ready for that daily jolt of Shiba fun (like a double espresso at early dawn!).

A COMMITTED NEW OWNER
By now you should understand what makes the Shiba Inu a most unique and special dog, one that will fit nicely into your family and lifestyle. If you have researched breeders, you should be able to recognize a knowledge-

SIGNS OF A HEALTHY PUPPY
Healthy puppies are robust little fellows who are alert and active, sporting shiny coats and supple skin. They should not appear lethargic, bloated or pot-bellied, nor should they have flaky skin or runny or crusted eyes or noses. Their stools should be firm and well formed, with no evidence of blood or mucus.

able and responsible Shiba Inu breeder who cares not only about his pups but also about what kind of owner you will be. If you have completed the final step in your new journey, you have found a litter, or possibly two, of quality Shiba pups.

A visit with the puppies and their breeder should be an education in itself. Breed research, breeder selection and puppy visitation are very important aspects of finding the puppy of your dreams. Beyond

TEMPERAMENT ABOVE ALL ELSE

Regardless of breed, a puppy's disposition is perhaps his most important quality. It is, after all, what makes a puppy lovable and "livable." If the puppy's parents or grandparents are known to be snappy or aggressive, the puppy is likely to inherit those tendencies. That can lead to serious problems, such as the dog's becoming a biter, which can lead to eventual abandonment.

that, these things also lay the foundation for a successful future with your pup. Puppy personalities within each litter vary, from the shy and easygoing puppy to the one who is dominant and assertive, with most pups falling somewhere in between. By spending time with the puppies you will be able to recognize certain behaviors and what these behaviors indicate about each pup's temperament. Which type of pup will complement your family dynamics is best determined by observing the puppies in action within their "pack." Remember that your breeder's expertise and recommendations are also valuable. Although you may fall in love with a bold and brassy male, the breeder may suggest that another pup would be best for you. The breeder's experience in rearing Shiba Inu pups and matching their temperaments with appropriate humans offers the best assurance that your pup will meet your needs and expectations. The type of puppy that you select is just as important as your decision that the Shiba Inu is the breed for you.

The decision to live with a Shiba is a serious commitment and not one to be taken lightly. This puppy is a living sentient being that will be dependent on you for basic survival for his entire life. Beyond the basics of survival—food, water, shelter and protection—he needs much, much more. The new pup needs love, nurturing and a proper canine education to mold him into a responsible, well-behaved canine citizen. Your Shiba Inu's health and good manners will need consistent monitoring and regular "tune-ups," so your job as a responsible dog owner will be ongoing throughout every stage of his life. If you are not prepared to accept these responsibilities and commit to them for the next decade, likely longer, then you are not prepared to own a dog of any breed.

Although the responsibilities of owning a dog may at times tax your patience, the joy of living with your Shiba Inu far outweighs the workload, and a well-mannered adult dog is worth your

time and effort. Before your very eyes, your new charge will grow up to be your most loyal friend, devoted to you unconditionally.

As irresistible as a fox pup, the Shiba puppy makes considerable demands on his owner's time, patience and lifestyle. Are you certain that you want this cunning fellow in your world?

YOUR SHIBA SHOPPING LIST

Just as expectant parents prepare a nursery for their baby, so should you ready your home for the arrival of your Shiba Inu pup. If you have the necessary puppy supplies purchased and in place before he comes home, it will ease the puppy's transition from the warmth and familiarity of his mom and littermates to the brand-new environment of his new home and human family. You will be too busy to stock up and prepare your house after your pup comes home, that's for sure! Imagine how a pup must feel upon being transported to a strange new place. It's up to you to comfort him and to let your little pup know that he is going to be happy with you.

THE WORRIES OF MANGE

Sometimes called "puppy mange," demodectic mange is passed to the puppy through the mother's milk. The microscopic mites that cause the condition take up residence in the puppy's hair follicles and sebaceous glands. Stress can cause the mites to multiply, causing bare patches on the face, neck and front legs. If neglected, it can lead to secondary bacterial infections, but if diagnosed and treated early, demodectic mange can be localized and controlled. Most pups recover without complications.

THE DOG CRATE

If you think that crates are tools of punishment and confinement for when a dog has misbehaved, think again. Most breeders and almost all trainers recommend a crate as the preferred house-training aid as well as for all-around puppy training and safety. Because dogs are natural den creatures that prefer cave-like environments, the benefits of crate use are many. The crate provides the puppy with his very own "safe house," a cozy place to sleep, take a break or seek comfort with a favorite toy; a travel aid to house your dog when on the road, at motels or at the vet's office; a training aid to help teach your puppy proper toileting habits; a

Meet the dam of your chosen Shiba puppy. Her physical appearance as well as temperament will be passed along to her pups.

FOOD AND WATER BOWLS

Your puppy will need separate bowls for his food and water. Stainless steel pans are generally preferred over plastic bowls since they sterilize better and pups are less inclined to chew on the metal. Heavy-duty ceramic bowls are popular, but consider how often you will have to pick up those heavy bowls. Buy adult-sized pans, as your puppy will grow into them before you know it.

DIGGING OUT

Some dogs love to dig. Others wouldn't think of it. Digging is considered "self-rewarding behavior" because it's fun! Of all the digging solutions offered by the experts, most are only marginally successful and none is guaranteed to work. The best cure is prevention, which means removing the dog from the offending site when he digs as well as distracting him when you catch him digging so that he turns his attentions elsewhere. That means that you have to supervise your dog's yard time. An unsupervised digger can create havoc with your landscaping or, worse, run away!

place of solitude when non-dog people happen to drop by and don't want a lively puppy—or even a well-behaved adult dog—saying hello or begging for attention.

Crates come in several types, although the wire crate and the fiberglass airline-type crate are the most popular. Shibas prefer the

> **CRATE EXPECTATIONS**
>
> To make the crate more inviting to your puppy, you can offer his first meal or two inside the crate, always keeping the crate door open so that he does not feel confined. Keep a favorite toy or two in the crate for him to play with while inside. You can also cover the crate at night with a lightweight sheet to make it more den-like and remove the stimuli of household activity. Never put him into his crate as punishment or as you are scolding him, since he will then associate his crate with negative situations and avoid going there.

wire crates because they offer better visibility as well as better ventilation. Shibas feel too important (nosy) to be content in enclosed fiberglass crates, though these are required for air travel. Many of the wire crates easily collapse into suitcase-size carriers. Furthermore, the fiberglass crates do not collapse and are less ventilated than a wire crate, which can be problematic in hot weather. Some of the newer crates are made of heavy plastic mesh; they are very lightweight and fold up into slim-line suitcases. However, a mesh crate might not be suitable for a pup with manic chewing habits.

A wire crate is the only choice for your Shiba's crate. Shibas need to know what is going on around them and will feel "trapped" in a fiberglass crate. When introduced to the crate as puppies, adult Shibas love to spend time in the comfort and security of their crates.

Although the Japanese-English dictionary doesn't agree, "Shiba" often translates to "mischief," as these busy pups demonstrate.

Don't bother with a puppy-sized crate. Although your Shiba Inu will be a wee fellow when you bring him home, he will grow up in the blink of an eye and your puppy crate will be useless. Purchase a crate that will accommodate an adult Shiba Inu. He will stand about 16 inches when full grown, so a medium-sized crate will fit him nicely.

A wire crate makes the best choice for a Shiba in the home.

BEDDING AND CRATE PADS

Your puppy will enjoy some type of soft bedding in his "room" (the crate), something he can snuggle into to feel cozy and secure. Old towels or blankets are good choices for a young pup, since he may (and probably will) have a toileting accident or two in the crate or decide to chew on the bedding material. Once he is fully trained and out of the early chewing stage, you can replace the puppy bedding with a permanent crate pad if you prefer. Crate pads and other dog beds run the gamut from inexpensive to high-end doggie-designer styles, but don't splurge on the good stuff until you are sure that your puppy is reliable and won't tear it up or make a mess on it.

PUPPY TOYS

Just as infants and older children require objects to stimulate their minds and bodies, puppies need toys to entertain their curious brains, wiggly paws and achy teeth. A fun array of safe doggie toys will help satisfy your puppy's chewing instincts and distract him from gnawing on the leg of your antique chair or your new leather sofa. Most puppy toys are cute and look as if they would be a lot of fun, but not all are necessarily safe or good for your puppy, so use caution when you go puppy-toy shopping.

Lambswool blankets can make a Shiba's bed or crate more cozy for the pup. These pups also think it is fun to play with.

Most Shibas are devoted chewers and like to sink their teeth in a good chew toy. The best "chewcifiers" are nylon and hard rubber bones; many are safe to gnaw on and come in sizes appropriate for all age groups and breeds. Be especially careful of natural bones, which can splinter or develop dangerous sharp edges; pups can easily swallow or choke on those bone splinters. Veterinarians often tell of surgical nightmares involving bits of splintered bone, because in addition to the danger of choking, the sharp pieces can damage the intestinal tract.

Shibas love squeaky and furry toys. Always supervise your pup whenever he has a toy that contains a squeaker, which could be dangerous if removed from the toy.

GOOD CHEWING

Chew toys run the gamut from rawhide chews to hard sterile bones and everything in between. Rawhides are all-time favorites, but they can cause choking when they become mushy from repeated chewing, causing them to break into small pieces that are easy to swallow. Rawhides are also highly indigestible, so many vets advise limiting rawhide treats. Hard sterile bones are great for plaque prevention as well as chewing satisfaction. Dispose of them when the ends become sharp or splintered.

TOYS 'R SAFE

The vast array of tantalizing puppy toys is staggering. Stroll through any pet shop or pet-supply outlet and you will see that the choices can be overwhelming. However, not all dog toys are safe or sensible. Most very young puppies enjoy soft woolly toys that they can snuggle with and carry around. (You know they have outgrown them when they shred them up!) Avoid toys that have buttons, tabs or other enhancements that can be chewed off and swallowed. Soft toys that squeak are fun, but make sure your puppy does not disembowel the toy and remove (and swallow) the squeaker. Toys that rattle or make noise can excite a puppy, but they present the same danger as the squeaky kind and so require supervision. Hard rubber toys that bounce can also entertain a pup, but make sure that the toy is too big for your pup to swallow.

Some Shibas are more orally fixated than others. A soft woolly toy (no matter how large) can be toted around all day by your happy Shiba.

Similarly, rawhide chews, while a favorite of most dogs and puppies, can be equally dangerous. Pieces of rawhide are easily swallowed after they get all gummy from chewing, and dogs have been known to choke on large pieces of ingested rawhide. Rawhide chews should be offered only when you can supervise the puppy.

Soft woolly toys are special Shiba favorites. They come in a wide variety of cute shapes and sizes; some look like little stuffed animals. Puppies love to shake them up and toss them about, or simply carry them around. Be careful of fuzzy toys that have button eyes or noses that your pup could chew off and swallow, and make sure that he does not disembowel a squeaky toy to remove the squeaker. Braided rope toys are similar in that they are fun to chew and toss around, but they shred easily and the strings are easy to swallow. The strings are not digestible and, if the puppy

Collaring Our Canines

The standard flat collar with a buckle or a snap, in leather, nylon or cotton, is widely regarded as the everyday all-purpose collar. If the collar fits correctly, you should be able to fit two fingers between the collar and the dog's neck.

Leather Buckle Collars

Limited-Slip Collar

The martingale, Greyhound or limited-slip collar is preferred by many dog owners and trainers. It is fixed with an extra loop that tightens when pressure is applied to the leash. The martingale collar gets tighter but does not "choke" the dog. The limited-slip collar should only be used for walking and training, not for free play or interaction with another dog. These types of collar should never be left on the dog, as the extra loop can lead to accidents.

Choke collars, usually made of stainless steel, are made for training purposes, though are not recommended for small dogs or heavily coated breeds. The chains can injure small dogs or damage long/abundant coats. Thin nylon choke leads are commonly used on show dogs while in the ring, though they are not practical for everyday use.

Snap Bolt Choke Collar

The harness, with two or three straps that attach over the dog's shoulders and around his torso, is a humane and safe alternative to the conventional collar. By and large, a well-made harness is virtually escape-proof. Harnesses are available in nylon and mesh and can be outfitted on most dogs, ranging from chest girths of 10 to 30 inches.

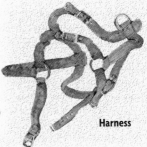

Harness

Nylon Collar

Quick-Click Closure

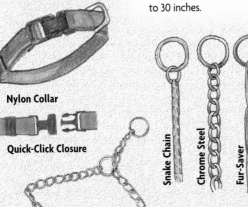

Snake Chain

Chrome Steel

Fur-Saver

Choke Chain Collars

A head collar, composed of a nylon strap that goes around the dog's muzzle and a second strap that wraps around his neck, offers the owner better control over his dog. This device is recommended for problem-solving with dogs (including jumping up, pulling and aggressive behaviors), but must be used with care.

A training halter, including a flat collar and two straps, made of nylon and webbing, is designed for walking. There are several on the market; some are more difficult to put on the dog than others. The halter harness, with two small slip rings at each end, is recommended for ease of use.

The selection of available puppy toys is immense, but not every toy is as well designed as it should be. Make sure that the ones you choose for your Shiba pup are safe.

often last very long, so be sure to remove and replace them when they get chewed up on the ends.

A word of caution about homemade toys: be careful with your choices of non-traditional play objects. Never use old shoes or socks, since a puppy cannot distinguish between the old ones on which he's allowed to chew and the new ones in your closet that are strictly off limits. That principle applies to anything that resembles something that you don't want your puppy to chew up.

doesn't pass them in his stool, he could end up at the vet's office. As with rawhides, your puppy should be closely monitored with rope toys.

If you believe that your pup has ingested one of these forbidden objects, check his stools for the next couple of days to see if he passes them when he defecates. At the same time, also watch for signs of intestinal distress. A call to your veterinarian might be in order to get his advice and be on the safe side.

An all-time favorite toy for puppies (young and old!) is the empty gallon milk jug. Hard plastic juice containers—46 ounces or more—are also excellent. Such containers make lots of noise when they are batted about, and puppies go crazy with delight as they play with them. However, they don't

FIRST CAR RIDE

The ride to your home from the breeder will no doubt be your puppy's first automobile experience, and you should make every effort to keep him comfortable and secure. Bring a large towel or small blanket for the puppy to lie on during the trip and an extra towel in case the pup gets carsick or has a potty accident. It's best to have another person with you to hold the puppy in his lap. Most puppies will fall fast asleep from the rolling motion of the car. If the ride is lengthy, you may have to stop so that the puppy can relieve himself, so be sure to bring a leash and collar for those stops. Avoid rest areas for potty trips, since those are frequented by many dogs, who may carry parasites or disease. It's better to stop at grassy areas near gas stations or shopping centers to prevent unhealthy exposure for your pup.

Leash Life

Dogs love leashes! Believe it or not, most dogs dance for joy every time their owners pick up their leashes. The leash means that the dog is going for a walk—and there are few things more exciting than that! Here are some of the kinds of leashes that are commercially available.

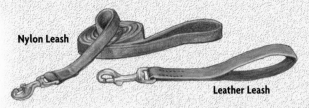

Nylon Leash

Leather Leash

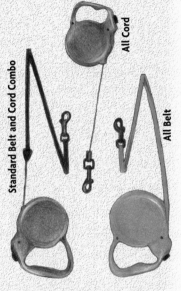

Standard Belt and Cord Combo

All Cord

All Belt

Retractable Leashes

Traditional Leash: Made of cotton, nylon or leather, these leashes are usually about 6 feet in length. A quality-made leather leash is softer on the hands than a nylon one. Durable woven cotton is a popular option. Lengths can vary up to about 48 feet, designed for different uses.

Chain Leash: Usually a metal chain leash with a plastic handle. This is not the best choice for most breeds, as it is heavier than other leashes and difficult to manage.

Retractable Leash: A long nylon cord is housed in a plastic device for extending and retracting. This leash, also known as a retractable leash, is ideal for taking trained dogs for long walks in open areas, although it is not recommended for large, powerful breeds. Different lengths and sizes are available, so check that you purchase one appropriate for your dog's weight.

Elastic Leash: A nylon leash with an elastic extension. This is useful for well-trained dogs, especially in conjunction with a head halter.

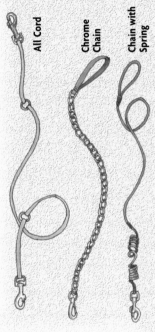

All Cord

Chrome Chain

Chain with Spring

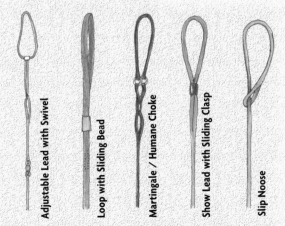

Adjustable Lead with Swivel

Loop with Sliding Bead

Martingale / Humane Choke

Show Lead with Sliding Clasp

Slip Noose

A Variety of Collar-Leash-in-One Products

Avoid leashes that are completely elastic, as they afford minimal control to the handler.

Adjustable Leash: This has two snaps, one on each end, and several metal rings. It is handy if you need to tether your dog temporarily, but is never to be used with a choke collar.

Tab Leash: A short leash (4 to 6 inches long) that attaches to your dog's collar. This device serves like a handle, in case you have to grab your dog while he's exercising off lead. It's ideal for "half-trained" dogs or dogs that listen only half the time.

Slip Leash: Essentially a leash with a collar built in, similar to what a dog-show handler uses to show a dog. This British-style collar has a ring on the end so that you can form a slip collar. Useful if you have to catch your own runaway dog or a stray.

COLLARS

A lightweight nylon collar is the best choice for a very young pup. Quick-clip collars are easy to put on and remove, and they can be adjusted as the puppy grows. Introduce him to his collar as soon as he comes home to get him accustomed to wearing it. He'll get used to it quickly and won't mind a bit. Make sure that it is snug enough that it won't slip off, yet loose enough to be comfortable for the pup. You should be able to slip two fingers between the collar and his neck. Check the collar often, as the puppy's neck and coat grow in spurts, and his collar can become too tight almost overnight. Choke collars are for training purposes only and should never be used on a puppy under four or five months old. Avoid chain choke collars on the Shiba, as they can damage the coat around the neck.

LEASHES

A 6-foot nylon lead is an excellent choice for a young puppy. It is lightweight and not as tempting to chew as a leather lead. You can switch to a 6-foot leather lead after your pup has grown and is used to walking politely on a lead. For initial puppy walks and house-training purposes, you should invest in a shorter lead so that you have more control over the puppy. At first, you don't want him wandering too far away

THE GRASS IS ALWAYS GREENER

Must dog owners decide between their beloved canine pals and their perfectly manicured emerald-green lawns? Just as dog urine is no tonic for growing grass, lawn chemicals are extremely dangerous to your dog. Fertilizers, pesticides and herbicides pose real threats to canines and humans alike. Dogs should be kept off treated grounds for at least 24 hours following treatment. Consider some organic options for your lawn care, such as using a homemade compost or a natural fertilizer instead of a commercial chemical. Some dog-conscious lawnkeepers avoid fertilizers entirely, keeping up their lawns by watering, aerating, mowing and seeding frequently.

As always, dogs complicate the equation. Canines love grass. They roll in it, eat it and love to bury their noses in it—and then do their business in it! Grass can mean hours of feel-good, smell-good fun! In addition to the dangers of lawn-care chemicals, there's also the threat of burs, thorns and pebbles in the grass, not to mention the very common grass allergy. Many dogs develop an incurably itchy skin condition from grass, especially in the late summer when the world is in full bloom.

from you, and when taking him out for toileting you will want to keep him in the specific area chosen for his potty spot.

Once the puppy is heel trained with a traditional leash, you can consider purchasing a retractable lead. A retractable lead is excellent for walking adult dogs that are already leash-wise. The retractable lead allows the dog to roam farther away from you and explore a wider area when out walking, and also retracts when you need to keep him close to you.

HOME SAFETY FOR YOUR PUPPY

The importance of puppy-proofing cannot be overstated. In addition to making your house comfortable for your Shiba Inu's arrival, you also must make sure that your house is safe for your puppy before you bring him home. There are countless hazards in the owner's personal living environment that a pup can sniff, chew, swallow or destroy. Many are obvious; others are not. Do a thorough advance house check to remove or rearrange those things that could hurt your puppy, keeping any potentially dangerous items out of areas to which he will have access.

Electrical cords are especially dangerous, since puppies view them as irresistible chew toys. Unplug and remove all exposed cords or fasten them beneath a baseboard where the puppy cannot reach them. Veterinarians and firefighters can tell you horror stories about electrical burns and house fires that resulted from puppy-chewed electrical cords. Consider this a most serious precaution for your puppy and the rest of your family.

Scout your home for tiny objects that might be seen at a pup's eye level. Keep medication bottles and cleaning supplies well out of reach, and do the same with waste baskets and other trash containers. It goes without saying that you should not use rodent poison or other toxic chemicals in any puppy area and that you must keep such containers safely locked up. You will be amazed at how many places a curious puppy can discover!

Once your house has cleared inspection, check your yard. A

KEEP OUT OF REACH

Most dogs don't browse around your medicine cabinet, but accidents do happen! The drug acetaminophen, the active ingredient in Tylenol®, can be deadly to dogs and cats if ingested in large quantities. Acetaminophen toxicity, caused by the dog's swallowing 15 to 20 tablets, can be manifested in abdominal pains within a day or two of ingestion, as well as liver damage. If you suspect your dog has swiped a bottle of Tylenol®, get the dog to the vet immediately so that the vet can induce vomiting and cleanse the dog's stomach.

sturdy fence, well embedded into the ground, will give your dog a safe place to play and potty. Check the fence periodically for necessary repairs. If there is a weak link or space to squeeze through, you can be sure a determined Shiba Inu will discover it. Remember that Shibas are celebrated escape artists and live to practice their art. Once a Shiba decides that it's time to find a way out, he will devote his entire spirit to the pursuit of freedom. Owners must be ready to prevent this escape and always have your sneakers handy!

The garage and shed can be hazardous places for a pup, as things like fertilizers, chemicals and tools are usually kept there. It's best to keep these areas off limits to the pup. Antifreeze is especially dangerous to dogs, as

TOXIC PLANTS
Plants are natural puppy magnets, but many can be harmful, even fatal, if ingested by a puppy or adult dog. Scout your yard and home interior and remove any plants, bushes or flowers that could be even mildly dangerous. It could save your puppy's life. You can obtain a complete list of toxic plants from your veterinarian, at the public library or by looking online.

they find the taste appealing and it takes only a few licks from the driveway to kill a dog, puppy or adult, small breed or large.

VISITING THE VETERINARIAN
A good veterinarian is your Shiba Inu puppy's best health insurance policy. If you do not already have a vet, ask friends and experienced dog people in your area for recommendations so that you can select a vet before you bring your Shiba Inu puppy home. Also arrange for your puppy's first veterinary examination beforehand, since many vets have two- and three-week waiting periods, and your puppy

Garages and outbuildings are prime sources of danger to the ever-busy Shiba Inu.

should visit the vet within a day or so of coming home.

It's important to make sure your puppy's first visit to the vet is a pleasant and positive one. The vet should take great care to befriend the pup and handle him gently to make their first meeting a positive experience. The vet will give the pup a thorough physical examination and set up a schedule for vaccinations and other necessary wellness visits. Be sure to show your vet any health and inoculation records, which you should have received from your breeder. Your vet is a great source of canine health information, so be sure to ask questions

Shibas are more than just curious; they are downright nosy. Don't let your Shiba pup do any unsupervised exploring.

and take notes. Creating a health journal for your puppy will make a handy reference for his wellness and any future health problems that may arise.

MEETING THE FAMILY

Your Shiba Inu's homecoming is an exciting time for all members of the family, and it's only natural that everyone will be eager to meet him, pet him and play with him. However, for the puppy's sake, it's best to make these initial family meetings as uneventful as possible so that the pup is not overwhelmed with too much too soon. Remember, he has just left his dam and his littermates and is away from the breeder's home for the first time. Despite his fuzzy wagging tail, he is still apprehensive and wondering where he is and who all these strange humans are. It's best to let him explore on his own and meet the family members as he feels

---

ASK THE VET

Help your vet help you to become a well-informed dog owner. Don't be shy about becoming involved in your puppy's veterinary care by asking questions and gaining as much knowledge as you can. For starters, ask what shots your puppy is getting and what diseases they prevent, and discuss with your vet the safest way to vaccinate. Find out what is involved in your dog's annual wellness visits. If you plan to spay or neuter, discuss the best age at which to have this done. Start out on the right "paw" with your puppy's vet and develop good communication with him, as he will care for your dog's health throughout the dog's entire life.

comfortable. Watch him as he investigates all the new smells, sights and sounds at his own pace. Children should be especially careful to not get overly excited, use loud voices or hug the pup too tightly. Be calm, gentle and affectionate, and be ready to comfort him if he appears frightened or uneasy.

Be sure to show your puppy his new crate during this first day home. Toss a treat or two inside the crate; if he associates the crate with food, he will associate the crate with good things. If he is comfortable with the crate, you can offer him his first meal inside it. Leave the door ajar so he can wander in and out as he chooses.

FIRST NIGHT IN HIS NEW HOME

So much has happened in your Shiba puppy's first day away from the breeder. He's had his first car ride to his new home. He's met his new human family and perhaps the other family pets. He has explored his new house and

> **PUPPY PARASITES**
> Parasites are nasty little critters that live in or on your dog or puppy. Most puppies are born with ascarid roundworms, which are acquired from dormant ascarids residing in the dam. Other parasites can be acquired through contact with infected fecal matter. Take a stool sample to your vet for testing. He will prescribe a safe wormer to treat any parasites found in your puppy's stool. Always have a fecal test performed at your puppy's annual veterinary exam.

yard, at least those places where he is to be allowed during his first weeks at home. He may have visited his new veterinarian. He has eaten his first meal or two away from his dam and litter-mates. Surely that's enough to tire out an eight-week-old Shiba Inu pup...or so you hope!

It's bedtime. During the day, the pup investigated his crate, which is his new den and sleeping space, so it is not entirely strange to him. Line the crate with a soft towel or blanket that he can snuggle into and gently place him into the crate for the night. Some breeders send home a piece of bedding from where the pup slept with his littermates, and those familiar scents are a great comfort for the puppy on his first night without his siblings.

Puppies learn the etiquette of social behavior from their dam and littermates. Rolling on your back tells your sibling that you're having a really good time!

He will probably whine or cry. The puppy is objecting to the confinement and the fact that he is alone for the first time. This can be a stressful time for you as well as for the pup. It's important that you remain resolute and don't let the puppy out of his crate to comfort him. He will fall asleep eventually. If you release him, the puppy will learn that crying means "out" and will continue that habit. You are laying the groundwork for future habits. Some breeders find that soft music can soothe a crying pup and help him get to sleep as well as drown out the whining.

SOCIALIZING YOUR PUPPY

The next 20 weeks of your Shiba puppy's life are the most important of his entire lifetime. A properly socialized puppy will grow up to be a confident and stable adult who will be a pleasure to live with and a welcome addition to the family.

The importance of socialization cannot be overemphasized. Research on canine behavior has proven that puppies who are not exposed to new sights, sounds, people and animals during their first 20 weeks of life will grow up to be timid and fearful, even aggressive, and unable to flourish outside their home environment.

Socializing your puppy is not difficult and, in fact, will be a fun

THE CRITICAL SOCIALIZATION PERIOD

Canine research has shown that a puppy's 8th through 16th week is the most critical learning period of his life. This is when the puppy "learns to learn," a time when he needs positive experiences to build confidence and stability. Puppies who are not exposed to different people and situations outside the home during this period can grow up to be fearful and sometimes aggressive. This is also the best time for puppy lessons, since he has not yet acquired any bad habits that could undermine his ability to learn.

time for you both. Lead training goes hand in hand with socialization, so your puppy will be learning how to walk on a lead at the same time that he's meeting the neighborhood. Because the Shiba Inu is a such a terrific breed, your puppy will enjoy being "the new *inu* on the block." Take him for short walks, to the park and to other dog-friendly places where he will encounter new people, especially children. Puppies automatically recognize children as "little people" and are drawn to play with them. Just make sure that you supervise these meetings and that the children do not get too rough or encourage him to play too hard. An overzealous pup can often nip too hard, frightening the child and in turn making the puppy overly excited. A bad experience in puppyhood can impact a dog for life, so a pup that has a negative experience with a child may grow up to be shy or even aggressive around children.

Take your puppy along on your daily errands. Puppies are natural "people magnets," and most people who see your pup will want to pet him. All of these

> **MAKE A COMMITMENT**
> Dogs are most assuredly man's best friend, but they are also a lot of work. When you add a puppy to your family, you also are adding to your daily responsibilities for years to come. Dogs need more than just food, water and a place to sleep. They also require training (which can be ongoing throughout the lifetime of the dog), activity to keep them physically and mentally fit and hands-on attention every day, plus grooming and health care. Your life as you now know it may well disappear! Are you prepared for such drastic changes?

Do not tolerate the puppy jumping up and chewing on your clothing. These type of cute antics lead to nuisance behavior as the puppy matures.

encounters will help to mold him into a confident adult dog. Likewise, you will soon feel like a confident, responsible dog owner, rightly proud of your handsome Shiba Inu.

Be especially careful of your puppy's encounters and experiences during the eight-to-ten-week-old period, which is also called the "fear period." This is a serious imprinting period, and all contact during this time should be gentle and positive. A frightening or negative event could leave a permanent impression that could affect his future behavior if a similar situation arises.

Also make sure that your puppy has received his first and second rounds of vaccinations before you expose him to other dogs or bring him to places that other dogs may frequent. Avoid dog parks and other strange-dog areas until your vet assures you that your puppy is fully immunized and resistant to the diseases that can be passed between canines. Discuss socialization with your breeder, as some breeders recommend socializing the puppy even before he has received all of his inoculations, depending on how outgoing the puppy may be.

LEADER OF THE PUPPY'S PACK

Like other canines, your puppy needs an authority figure, someone he can look up to and regard as the leader of his "pack." His first pack leader was his dam, who taught him to be polite and not chew too hard on her ears or nip at her muzzle. He learned those same lessons from his littermates. If he played too rough, they cried in pain and stopped the game, which sent an important message to the rowdy puppy.

As puppies play together, they are also struggling to determine who will be the boss. Being pack animals, dogs need someone to be in charge. If a litter of puppies remained together beyond puppyhood, one of the pups would emerge as the strongest one, the one who calls the shots.

Once your puppy leaves the pack, he will look intuitively for a new leader. If he does not

SOME DAM ATTITUDE
When selecting a puppy, be certain to meet the dam of the litter. The temperament of the dam is often predictive of the temperament of her puppies. However, dams occasionally are very protective of their young, some to the point of being testy or aggressive with visitors, whom they may view as a danger to their babies. Such attitudes are more common when the pups are very young and still nursing and should not be mistaken for actual aggressive temperament. If possible, visit the dam away from her pups to make friends with her and gain a better understanding of her true personality.

recognize you as that leader, he will try to assume that position for himself. Of course, it is hard to imagine your adorable Shiba Inu puppy trying to be in charge when he is so small and seemingly helpless. You must remember that these are natural canine instincts. Do not cave in and allow your pup to get the upper "paw"!

Just as socialization is so important during these first 20 weeks, so too is your puppy's early education. He was born without any bad habits. He does not know what is good or bad behavior. If he does things like nipping and digging, it's because he is having fun and doesn't know that humans consider those things as "bad." It's your job to teach him proper puppy manners, and this is the best time to accomplish

ROCK-A-BYE BEDDING

The wide assortment of dog beds today can make your choice quite difficult, as there are many adorable novelty beds in fun styles and prints. It's wise to wait until your puppy has outgrown the chewing stage before providing him with a dog bed, since he might make confetti out of it. Your puppy will be happy with an old towel or blanket in his crate until he is old enough to resist the temptation to chew up his bed. For a dog of any age, a bed with a washable cover is always a wise choice.

that...before he has developed bad habits, since it is much more difficult to "unlearn" or correct unacceptable learned behavior than to teach good behavior from the start.

Make sure that all members of the family understand the importance of being consistent when training their new puppy. If you tell the puppy to stay off the sofa and your daughter allows him to cuddle on the couch to watch her favorite television show, your pup will be confused about what he is and is not allowed to do. Have a family conference before your pup comes home so that everyone understands the basic principles of puppy training and the rules you have set forth for the pup, and agrees to follow them.

The old adage that "an ounce of prevention is worth a pound of cure" is especially true when it comes to puppies. It is much easier to prevent inappropriate behavior than it is to change it. It's also easier and less stressful for the pup, since it will keep discipline to a minimum and create a more positive learning environment for him. That, in turn, will also be easier on you!

SOLVING PUPPY PROBLEMS

CHEWING AND NIPPING
Nipping at fingers and toes is normal puppy behavior. Chewing

is also the way that puppies investigate their surroundings. However, you will have to teach your puppy that chewing anything other than his toys is not acceptable. That won't happen overnight, and at times puppy teeth will test your patience. However, if you allow nipping and chewing to continue, just think about the damage that a mature Shiba Inu can do with a full set of adult teeth.

Whenever your puppy nips your hand or fingers, cry out "Ouch!" in a loud voice, which should startle your puppy and stop him from nipping, even if only for a moment. Immediately distract him by offering a small treat or an appropriate toy for him to chew instead (which means having chew toys and puppy treats handy or in your pockets at all times). Praise him when he takes the toy and tell him what a good fellow he is. Praise is just as or even more important in puppy training as discipline and correction.

Puppies also tend to nip at children more often than adults, since they perceive little ones to be more vulnerable and more similar to their littermates. Teach your children appropriate responses to nipping behavior. If they are unable to handle it themselves, you may have to intervene. Puppy nips can be quite painful and a child's fright-

Shiba puppies look for attention and crave the center stage spotlight. Don't spoil your puppy or you'll soon have a major diva on your hands.

ened reaction will only encourage a puppy to nip harder, which is a natural canine response. As with all other puppy situations, interaction between your Shiba Inu puppy and children should be supervised.

Chewing on objects, not just family members' fingers and ankles, is also normal canine behavior that can be especially tedious (for the owner, not the pup) during the teething period when the puppy's adult teeth are coming in. At this stage, chewing just plain feels good. Furniture legs and cabinet corners are common puppy favorites. Shoes and other personal items also taste pretty good to a pup.

The best solution is, once again, prevention. If you value something, keep it tucked away and out of reach. You can't hide your dining-room table in a closet, but you can try to deflect the chewing by applying a bitter product made just to deter dogs from chewing. Available in a spray or cream, this substance is vile-tasting, although safe for dogs, and most puppies will avoid the forbidden object after one tiny taste. You also can apply the product to your leather leash if the puppy tries to chew on his lead during leash-training sessions.

Keep a ready supply of safe chews handy to offer your Shiba Inu as a distraction when he starts to chew on something that's a "no-no." Remember, at this tender age he does not yet know what is permitted or forbidden, so you have to be "on call" every minute he's awake and on the prowl.

You may lose a treasure or two during puppy's growing-up period, and the furniture could sustain a nasty nick or two. These can be trying times, so be prepared for those inevitable accidents and comfort yourself in knowing that this too shall pass.

PUPPY WHINING

Puppies often cry and whine, just as infants and little children do. It's their way of telling us that they are lonely or in need of attention. Your puppy will miss his littermates and will feel insecure when he is left alone. You may be out of the house or just in another room, but he will still feel alone. During these times, the puppy's crate should be his personal comfort station, a place all his own where he can feel safe and secure. Once he learns that being alone is okay and not

something to be feared, he will settle down without crying or objecting. You might want to leave a radio on while he is crated, as the sound of human voices can be soothing and will give the impression that people are around.

Give your puppy a favorite cuddly toy or chew toy to entertain him whenever he is crated. You will both be happier: the puppy because he is safe in his den and you because he is quiet, safe and not getting into puppy escapades that can wreak havoc in your house or cause him danger.

To make sure that your puppy will always view his crate as a safe and cozy place, never, ever, use the crate as punishment. That's the best way to turn the crate into a negative place that the pup will want to avoid. Sure, you can use the crate for your own peace of mind if your puppy is getting into trouble and needs some "time out." Just don't let him know that! Never scold the pup and immediately place him into the crate. Count to ten, give him a couple of hugs and maybe a treat, then scoot him into his crate.

It's also important not to make a big fuss when he is released from the crate. That will make getting out of the crate more appealing than being in the crate, which is just the opposite of what you are trying to achieve.

PROPER CARE OF YOUR

SHIBA INU

Adding a Shiba Inu to your household means adding a new family member who will need your care each and every day. When your Shiba Inu pup first comes home, you will start a routine with him so that as he grows up your dog will have a daily schedule just as you do. The aspects of your dog's daily care will likewise become regular parts of your day, so you'll both have a new schedule. Dogs learn by consistency and thrive on routine: regular times for meals, exercise, grooming and potty trips are just as important for your dog as they are to you. Your dog's schedule will depend much on your family's daily routine, but remember that you now have a new member of the family who is part of your day every day.

FEEDING

Feeding your Shiba the best diet is based primarily on various factors, including age, activity level and overall condition. When you visit the breeder, he will share with you his advice about the proper diet for your dog based on his experience with the breed and the foods with which he has had success. Likewise, your vet will be a helpful source of advice throughout the dog's life and will aid you in planning a diet for optimal health.

FEEDING THE PUPPY

Of course, your pup's very first food will be his dam's milk. There may be special situations in which pups fail to nurse, necessitating that the breeder hand-feed them with a formula, but for the most part pups spend the first weeks of life nursing from their dam. The breeder weans the pups by gradually introducing solid foods and decreasing the milk meals. Pups may even start themselves off on the weaning process, albeit inadvertently, if they snatch bites from their mom's food bowl.

By the time the pups are ready for new homes, they are

Feeding time at the breeder's establishment is a communal affair.

DIET DON'TS

- Got milk? Don't give it to your dog! Dogs cannot tolerate large quantities of cows' milk, as they do not have the enzymes to digest lactose.
- You may have heard of dog owners who add raw eggs to their dogs' food for a shiny coat or to make the food more palatable, but consumption of raw eggs too often can cause a deficiency of the vitamin biotin.
- Avoid feeding table scraps, as they will upset the balance of the dog's complete food. Additionally, fatty or highly seasoned foods can cause upset canine stomachs.
- Do not offer raw meat to your dog. Raw meat can contain parasites; it also is high in fat.
- Vitamin A toxicity in dogs can be caused by too much raw liver, especially if the dog already gets enough vitamin A in his balanced diet, which should be the case.
- Bones like chicken, pork chop and other soft bones are not suitable, as they easily splinter.

Improper diet and exercise habits can lead to damaging problems that will compromise the dog's health and movement for his entire life. That being said, new owners should not worry needlessly. With the myriad types of food formulated specifically for growing pups of different-sized breeds, dog-food manufacturers have taken much of the guesswork out of feeding your puppy well. Since growth-food formulas are designed to provide the nutrition that a growing puppy needs, it is unnecessary and, in fact, can prove harmful to add supplements to the diet. Research has shown that too much of certain vitamin supplements and minerals predispose a dog to skeletal problems. It's by no means a case of "if a little is good, a lot is better." At every stage of your dog's life, too much or too little in the way of nutrients can be harmful, which is why a manufactured complete food is the easiest way to know that your dog is getting what he needs.

Because of a young pup's small body and accordingly small digestive system, his daily portion will be divided up into small meals throughout the day. This can mean starting off with three or more meals a day and decreasing the number of meals as the pup matures. Eventually you can feed only one meal a day, although it is generally thought that dividing

fully weaned and eating a good puppy food. As a new owner, you may be thinking, "Great! The breeder has taken care of the hard part." Not so fast.

A puppy's first year of life is the time when all or most of his growth and development takes place. This is a delicate time, and diet plays a huge role in proper skeletal and muscular formation.

the day's food into two meals on a morning/evening schedule is healthier for the dog's digestion.

Regarding the feeding schedule, feeding the pup at the same times and in the same place each day is important for both housebreaking purposes and establishing the dog's everyday routine. As for the amount to feed, growing puppies generally need proportionately more food per body weight than their adult counterparts, but a pup should never be allowed to gain excess weight. Dogs of all ages should be kept in proper body condition, but extra weight can strain a pup's developing frame, causing skeletal problems.

Watch your pup's weight as he grows and, if the recommended amounts seem to be too much or too little for your pup, consult the vet about appropriate dietary changes. Keep in mind that treats, although small, can quickly add up throughout the day, contributing unnecessary calories. Treats are fine when used prudently; opt for dog treats specially formulated to be healthy or for nutritious snacks like small pieces of cheese or cooked chicken.

FEEDING THE ADULT DOG

For the adult (meaning physically mature) dog, feeding properly is about maintenance, not growth. Again, correct weight is a concern. Your dog should appear fit and should have an evident "waist." His ribs should not be protruding (a sign of being underweight), but they should be covered by only a slight layer of fat. Under normal circumstances, an adult dog can be maintained fairly easily with a high-quality nutritionally complete adult-formula food.

Factor treats into your dog's

JUST ADD MEAT

An organic alternative to the traditional dog kibble or canned food comes in the form of grain-based feeds. These dry cereal-type products consist of oat and rye flakes, corn meal, wheat germ, dried kelp and other natural ingredients. The manufacturers recommend that the food be mixed with meat in a ratio of two parts grain to one part meat. As an alternative to fresh meat, investigate freeze-dried meat and fermented meat products, which makers claim are more nutritious and digestible for dogs.

NOT HUNGRY?

No dog in his right mind would turn down his dinner, would he? If you notice that your dog has lost interest in his food, there could be any number of causes. Dental problems are a common cause of appetite loss, one that is often overlooked. If your dog has a toothache, a loose tooth or sore gums from infection, chances are it doesn't feel so good to chew. Think about when you've had a toothache! If your dog does not approach the food bowl with his usual enthusiasm, look inside his mouth for signs of a problem. Whatever the cause, you'll want to consult your vet so that your chow hound can get back to his happy, hungry self as soon as possible.

overall daily caloric intake, and avoid offering table scraps. Overweight dogs are more prone to health problems. Research has even shown that obesity takes years off a dog's life. With that in mind, resist the urge to overfeed

and over-treat. Don't make unnecessary additions to your dog's diet, whether with tidbits or with extra vitamins and minerals.

The amount of food needed for proper maintenance will vary depending on the individual dog's activity level, but you will be able to tell whether the daily portions are keeping him in good shape. With the wide variety of good complete foods available, choosing what to feed is largely a matter of personal preference. Just as with the puppy, the adult dog should have consistency in his mealtimes and feeding place. In addition to a consistent routine, regular mealtimes also allow the owner to see how much his dog is eating. If the dog seems never to be satisfied or, likewise, becomes uninterested in his food, the owner will know right away that something is wrong and can consult the vet.

DIETS FOR THE AGING DOG

A good rule of thumb is that once a dog has reached 75% of his expected lifespan, he has reached "senior citizen" or geriatric status. Your Shiba Inu will be considered a senior at about 9 years of age; based on his size, he has a projected lifespan of about 12–14 years.

What does aging have to do with your dog's diet? No, he won't get a discount at the local diner's early-bird special. Yes, he will

A nursing dam will have different nutritional requirements from other dogs. Discuss the diet of your Shiba with your vet as well as your breeder.

require some dietary changes to accommodate the changes that come along with increased age. One change is that the older dog's dietary needs become more similar to those of a puppy. Specifically, dogs can metabolize more protein as youngsters and seniors than in the adult-maintenance stage. Discuss with your vet whether you need to switch to a higher-protein or senior-formulated food or whether your current adult-dog food contains sufficient nutrition for the senior.

Watching the dog's weight remains essential, even more so in the senior stage. Older dogs are already more vulnerable to illness, and obesity only contributes to their susceptibility to problems.

VARIETY IS THE SPICE

Although dog-food manufacturers contend that dogs don't like variety in their diets, studies show quite the opposite to be true. Dogs would much rather vary their meals than eat the same old chow day in and day out. Dry kibble is no more exciting for a dog than the same bowl of bran flakes would be for you. Fortunately, there are dozens of varieties available on the market, and your dog will likely show preference for certain flavors over others. A word of warning: don't overdo it or you'll develop a fussy eater who only prefers chopped beef fillet and asparagus tips every night.

As the older dog becomes less active and thus exercises less, his regular portions may cause him to gain weight. At this point, you may consider decreasing his daily food intake or switching to a reduced-calorie food. As with other changes, you should consult your vet for advice.

TYPES OF FOOD AND READING THE LABEL

When selecting the type of food to feed your dog, it is important to check out the label for ingredients. Many dry-food products have soybean, corn or rice as the main ingredient. The main ingredient will be listed first on the label, with the rest of the ingredients following in descending order according to their proportion in the food. While these types of dry food are fine, you should also look into dry foods based on meat or fish. These are better-quality foods and thus higher priced. However, they may be just as economical in the long run, because studies have shown that it takes less of the higher-quality foods to maintain a dog.

Comparing the various types of food, dry, canned and semi-moist, dry foods contain the least amount of water and canned foods the most. Proportionately, dry foods are the most calorie- and nutrient-dense, which means that you need more of a canned food product to supply the same

FEEDING THE SHIBA COAT

How much does your Shiba's diet affect his coat? As master Akita breeder B.J. Andrews tells us, "First you breed a coat and then you feed a coat." In addition to offering your Shiba top-quality dry food, you can add some secret ingredients to help your Shiba develop a shimmering full coat that would make a Husky blush. Add seaweed kelp to your dog's food ration. Japanese dogs thrive on foods from the sea. Offer your Shiba some fresh white fish, crab or caviar as a treat and watch him come to life. Another secret the author learned from Shiba breeder Rick Tomita is to add a small amount of mink food to your Shiba's bowl. (Have you ever seen a lackluster mink?) You can mail-order mink food from the Internet.

amount of nutrition. In households domiciling breeds of disparate size, the canned/dry/semi-moist question can be of special importance. Larger breeds obviously eat more than smaller ones and thus in general do better on dry foods, but smaller breeds like the Shiba do fine on canned foods and require "small bite" formulations to protect their small mouths and teeth if fed only dry foods. So if you have breeds of different size in your household, consider both your own preferences and what your dogs like to eat, but in the main think canned for the little guys and dry or semi-moist for everyone else. You may find success mixing the food types as well. Water is important for all dogs, but even more so for those fed dry foods, as there is minimal water content in their food.

There are strict controls that regulate the nutritional content of dog food, and a food has to meet the minimum requirements in order to be considered "complete and balanced." It is important that you choose such a food for your dog, so check the label to be sure that your chosen food meets the requirements. If not, look for a food that clearly states on the label that it is formulated to be complete and balanced for your dog's particular stage of life.

Recommendations for amounts to feed will also be indicated on the label. You should also ask your vet about proper food portions, and you will keep an eye on your dog's condition to see whether the recommended amounts are adequate. If he becomes over- or underweight, you will need to make adjustments; this also would be a good time to consult your vet.

The food label may also make feeding suggestions, such as whether moistening a dry-food product is recommended. Sometimes a splash of water will make the food more palatable for the dog and even enhance the

SWITCHING FOODS

There are certain times in a dog's life when it becomes necessary to switch his food; for example, from puppy to adult food and then from adult to senior-dog food. Additionally, you may decide to feed your pup a different type of food from what he received from the breeder, and there may be "emergency" situations in which you can't find your dog's normal brand and have to offer something else temporarily. Anytime a change is made, for whatever reason, the switch must be done gradually. You don't want to upset the dog's stomach or end up with a picky eater who refuses to eat something new. A tried-and-true approach is, over the course of about a week, to mix a little of the new food in with the old, increasing the proportion of new to old as the days progress. At the end of the week, you'll be feeding his regular portions of the new food, and he will barely notice the change!

flavor. Don't be overwhelmed by the many factors that go into feeding your dog. Manufacturers of complete and balanced foods make it easy, and once you find the right food and amounts for your Shiba Inu, his daily feeding will be a matter of routine.

Don't Forget the Water!

Regardless of what type of food he eats, there's no doubt that he needs plenty of water. Fresh cold water, in a clean bowl, should be freely available to your dog at all times. There are special circumstances, such as during puppy housebreaking, when you will want to monitor your pup's water intake so that you will be able to predict when he will need to relieve himself, but water must be available to him nonetheless. Water is essential for hydration and proper body function just as it is in humans.

You will get to know how much your dog typically drinks in a day. Of course, in the heat or if exercising vigorously, he will be more thirsty and will drink more. However, if he begins to drink noticeably more water for no apparent reason, this could signal any of various problems, and you are advised to consult your vet.

Water is the best drink for dogs. Some owners are tempted to give milk from time to time or to moisten dry food with milk, but dogs do not have the enzymes necessary to digest the lactose in milk, which is much different from the milk that nursing

Offer your adult Shiba fresh, clean water all day long. If your Shiba is drinking excessively, you should consult your vet.

TWO'S COMPANY

One surefire method of increasing your adult dog's exercise plan is to adopt a second dog. If your dog is well socialized, he should take to his new canine pal in no time and soon the two will be giving each other lots of activity and exercise as they play, romp and explore together. Most owners agree that two dogs are hardly much more work than one. If you cannot afford a second dog, get together with a friend or neighbor who has a well-trained dog. Your dog will definitely enjoy the company of a new four-legged playmate.

puppies receive. Therefore stick with clean fresh water to quench your dog's thirst, and always have it readily available to him.

EXERCISE

The Shiba challenge is keeping up with this active little spitz dog! A Shiba is always ready for a walk and, in cool weather, will welcome an hour's walk with his owner once or twice a day! If you are fortunate to have a sizeable yard, the Shiba will enjoy running and playing for hours each day. Shibas will play with their owners, chasing a ball, flying disk or some other favorite toy. Perhaps the best exercise for the Shiba is another Shiba! The author solved his Shiba exercise and entertainment problem by

acquiring a second Shiba within six months of his first Shiba. Male and female Shibas can be best of friends and love the time they spend chasing each other and playing. Fighting over toys and fetching toys with their owners are marvelous exercise for these feisty Nipponese wonders.

For their size, Shibas require considerable exercise. They can keep up with an owner on his morning jog and can even run alongside a bicycle for a not-too-long ride on a cool day. Avoid too much exercise in hot weather. These are Nordic dogs that prefer the cooler climes. Shibas can overheat in their enthusiasm to keep up with their owner or another dog.

Not only is exercise essential to keep the dog's body fit, it is essential to his mental well-being. A bored Shiba will find something to do, which often manifests itself in some type of destructive behavior. A Shiba left outside without toys or stimulation will dig holes, eat shrubs or escape. Fortunately, Shibas like toys and bones and can occupy themselves for hours. Do not give your Shiba opportunity to hone its creative resources. You will be sorry. Provide the Shiba with ample exercise, toys for amusement and lots of attention and he will be happy and well behaved.

WEIGHT AND SEE!

When you look at yourself in the mirror each day, you get very used to what you see! It's only when you pull out last year's summer suit and can't zipper it that you notice that you've put on some pounds. Dog owners are the same way with their dogs. Often a few pounds go unnoticed, and it's not until some time passes or the vet remarks that your dog looks more than pleasantly plump that you realize what's happened. To avoid your pet's becoming obese right under your very nose, make a habit of routinely evaluating his condition with a hands-on test.

Can you feel, but not see, your dog's rib cage? Does your dog have a waist? His waist should be evident by touch and also visible from above and from the side. In top view, the dog's body should have an hourglass shape. These are indicators of good condition.

While it's not hard to spot an extremely skinny or overly rotund dog, it's the subtle changes that lead up to under- or overweight condition of which we must be aware. If your dog's ribs are visible, he is too thin. Conversely, if you can't feel the ribs under too much fat, and if there's no indication of a waistline, your dog is overweight. Both of these conditions require changes to the diet. A trip or sometimes just a call to the vet will help you modify your dog's feeding.

GROOMING

BRUSHING

Shibas do not require too much grooming time of their owners, except during their biannual coat casting. During the shedding season, the Shiba will blow his whole undercoat, the white fluffy down coat that gives the Shiba coat its fullness. Owners will need to brush the coat twice a day for about two weeks during these periods. During the other months of the year, the Shiba can be given a quick once-over each week. A soft bristle or slicker brush is ideal as well as a wide-toothed metal comb. Brush the whole coat, including the chest, underparts and tail. If introduced to brushing as a pup, most Shibas do not mind being groomed and enjoy the attention from their fawning owners.

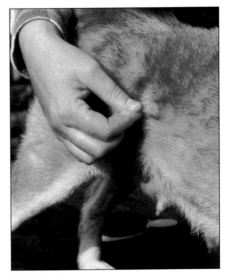

The Shiba has a double coat, consisting of a hard outer layer of hair and a soft, cottony undercoat. When a Shiba sheds twice annually, the undercoat becomes loose and requires twice daily grooming.

This lovely dam has graciously agreed to model for the grooming photos. The Shiba coat requires regular grooming to keep looking shiny and clean.

During shedding season, a slicker brush or rake works efficiently to remove the dead undercoat.

Misting the coat during grooming sessions keeps the coat moist and avoids hairs from breaking.

BATHING

Brushing is one thing…but don't say the word B-A-T-H! Most Shibas do not welcome the idea of bathing! Getting wet and being a Shiba do not complement one another. You will have to introduce the Shiba to bathing early on. Most Shibas scream the first time water touches their coats. Be prepared and be the top dog. Talk your Shiba through it with gentle encouragement and a strong grip. Even though your Shiba puppy may weigh only a few pounds, get a friend to help you bathe the dog the first time. You will need the extra hands to keep the Shiba under control.

Fortunately, dogs do not need to be bathed as often as humans, but regular bathing is essential for healthy skin and a healthy, shiny coat. Brush your Shiba thoroughly before wetting his coat. Make certain that your dog has a good non-slip surface to stand on. Begin by wetting the dog's coat. A shower or hose attachment is necessary for thoroughly wetting and rinsing the coat. Check the water temperature to make sure that it is neither too hot nor too cold.

Next, apply shampoo to the dog's coat and work it into a good lather. You should purchase a shampoo that is made for dogs. Do not use a product made for human hair. Wash the head last; you do not want shampoo to drip into the dog's eyes while you are washing the rest of his body. Shibas hate water near their ears, so be especially careful. Work the shampoo all the way down to the skin. You can use this opportunity to check the skin for any bumps, bites or other abnormalities. Do not neglect any area of the body—get all of the hard-to-reach places.

Once the dog has been thoroughly shampooed, he requires an equally thorough rinsing. Shampoo left in the coat

The Shiba's hindquarters should be attended to in order to create a proper full skirt (pantaloons on a dog!).

When trained from puppyhood, the Shiba stands still and patiently during her salon appointment.

Don't forget to brush the tail to keep it plush and free from debris or loose hairs. It is a key component in the Shiba's appearance.

WATER SHORTAGE

No matter how well behaved your dog is, bathing is always a project! Nothing can substitute for a good warm bath, but owners do have the option of giving their dogs "dry" baths. Pet shops sell excellent products, in both powder and spray forms, designed for spot-cleaning your dog. These dry shampoos are convenient for touch-up jobs when you don't have the time to bathe your dog in the traditional way.

Muddy feet, messy behinds and smelly coats can be spot-cleaned and deodorized with a "wet-nap"-style cleaner. On those days when your dog insists on rolling in fresh goose droppings and there's no time for a bath, a spot bath can save the day. These pre-moistened wipes are also handy for other grooming needs like wiping faces, ears and eyes and freshening tails and behinds.

PRESERVING THOSE PEARLY WHITES

Pet shops sell terrific tooth-care devices, including specially designed toothbrushes, yummy toothpastes and finger-model brushes. You can use a human toothbrush with soft bristles, but never use human toothpastes, which can damage the dog's enamel. Baking soda is an alternative to doggy toothpastes, but your dog will be more receptive to canine toothpastes with the flavor of liver or hamburger. Make tooth care fun for your dog. Let him think that you're "horsing around" with his mouth. When brushing the dog's teeth, begin with the largest teeth (the canines) and proceed back toward the molars.

Ear problems are not uncommon in the Shiba. Cleaning the ears with a simple solution of hydrogen peroxide and white vinegar will keep the ears mite- and wax-free.

Be prepared for your dog to shake out his coat—you might want to stand back, but make sure you have a hold on the dog to keep him from running through the house. Since this is such an ordeal for most Shibas, it pays to repeat the shampooing process before drying the dog.

EAR CLEANING

The ears should be kept clean with a cotton ball and ear powder made especially for dogs. Be on the lookout for any signs of infection or ear mite infestation, which are too common in Shibas. If your Shiba Inu has been shaking his head or scratching at his ears frequently, this usually indicates a problem. If his ears have an unusual odor, this is a sure sign of mite infestation or infection, and a signal to have his ears checked by the veterinarian.

can be irritating to the skin. Protect his eyes from the shampoo by shielding them with your hand and directing the flow of water in the opposite direction. You should also avoid getting water in the ear canal.

THE MONTHLY GRIND

If your dog doesn't like the feeling of nail clippers or if you're not comfortable using them, you may wish to try an electric nail grinder. This tool has a small sandpaper disc on the end that rotates to grind the nails down. Some feel that using a grinder reduces the risk of cutting into the quick; this can be true if the tool is used properly. Usually you will be able to tell where the quick is before you get to it. A benefit of the grinder is that it creates a smooth finish on the nails so that there are no ragged edges.

Shibas hate having their ears touched, but cleaning the ears will prevent having to cure a mite problem later on.

NAIL CLIPPING

Having his nails trimmed is not on many dogs' lists of favorite things to do. With this in mind, you will need to accustom your puppy to the procedure at a young age so that he will sit still (well, as still as he can) for his pedicures. Long nails can cause the dog's feet to spread, which is not good for him; likewise, long nails can hurt if they unintentionally scratch, not good for you!

Some dogs' nails are worn down naturally by regular walking on hard surfaces, so the frequency with which you clip depends on your individual dog.

Look at his nails from time to time and clip as needed; a good way to know when it's time for a trim is if you hear your dog clicking as he walks across the floor.

There are several types of nail clippers and even electric nail-grinding tools made for dogs; first we'll discuss using the clipper. To start, have your clipper ready and some doggie treats on hand. You want your pup to view his nail-clipping sessions in a positive light, and what better way to convince him than with food? You may want to enlist the help of an assistant to comfort the pup and offer treats as you concentrate on the clipping itself. The guillotine-type clipper is thought of by many as the easiest type to use; the nail tip is inserted into the opening, and blades on the top and bottom snip it off in one clip.

Easy does it when using the nail clipper; remove just a small portion of the nail with each clip.

Start by grasping the pup's paw; a little pressure on the foot pad causes the nail to extend, making it easier to clip. Clip off a little at a time. If you can see the "quick," which is a blood vessel that runs through each nail, you will know how much to trim, as you do not want to cut into the quick. On that note, if you do cut the quick, which will cause bleeding, you can stem the flow of blood with a styptic pencil or other clotting agent. If you mistakenly nip the quick, do not panic or fuss, as this will cause the pup to be afraid. Simply reassure the pup, stop the bleeding and move on to the next nail. Don't be discouraged; you will become a professional canine pedicurist with practice.

You may or may not be able to see the quick, so it's best to just clip off a small bit at a time. If you see a dark dot in the center of the nail, this is the quick and your cue to stop clipping. Tell the puppy he's a "good boy" and offer a piece of treat with each nail. You can also use nail-clipping time to examine the footpads, making sure that they are not dry and cracked and that nothing has become embedded in them.

The nail grinder, the second choice, is many owners' first choice. Accustoming the puppy to the sound of the grinder and sensation of the buzz presents fewer challenges than the clipper, and there's little chance of cutting through the quick. Use the grinder on a low setting and always talk soothingly to your dog. He won't mind his salon visit, and he'll have nicely polished nails as well.

EYE CARE

During grooming sessions, pay extra attention to the condition of your dog's eyes. If the area around the eyes is soiled or if tear staining has occurred, there are various cleaning agents made especially for this purpose. Look at the dog's eyes to make sure no debris has entered; dogs who spend time outdoors are especially prone to this.

The signs of an eye infection are obvious: mucus, redness, puffiness, scabs or other signs of irritation. If your dog's eyes become infected, the vet will likely prescribe an antibiotic ointment for treatment. If you notice signs of more serious problems, such as opacities in the eye, which usually indicate cataracts, consult the vet at once. Taking time to pay attention to your dog's eyes will alert you in the early stages of any problem so that you can get your dog treatment as soon as possible. You could save your dog's sight!

IDENTIFICATION AND TRAVEL

IDENTIFICATION

Your Shiba Inu is your valued companion and friend who likes to run away! That is why you always keep two very close eyes on him at all times and why you have made sure that he cannot escape from the yard or wriggle out of his collar and run away from you. However, when it comes to Shibas, escape is a part of life and accidents can happen. If this unfortunate event should occur, the first thing on your mind will be finding him. Proper identification, including an ID tag, a tattoo and possibly a microchip, will increase the chances of his being returned to you safely and

quickly. This is not an option for Shiba owners—it is a "must." It pays to be prepared. Your neighbors are vital in helping you keep your Shiba alive and safe. Since the breed is so appealing and eye-catching, your neighbors will likely recognize the little tyke as yours. It pays to be considerate and friendly to all your neighbors as they can be part of your regular Shiba search crew.

HIT THE ROAD

Car travel with your Shiba Inu may be limited to necessity only, such as trips to the vet, or you may bring your dog along almost everywhere you go. This will depend much on your individual dog and how he reacts to rides in

The only safe way to travel with a Shiba is in her crate. Although Shibas would much rather be smelling the breeze through the window or licking the windshield, they belong safely stowed in their crates.

the car. You can begin desensitizing your dog to car travel as a pup so that it's something that he's used to. Still, some dogs suffer from motion sickness. Your vet may prescribe a medication for this if trips in the car pose a problem for your

dog. At the very least, you will need to get him to the vet, so he will need to tolerate these trips with the least amount of hassle possible.

Start taking your pup on short trips, maybe just around the block to start. If he is fine with short trips, lengthen your rides a little at a time. Start to take him on your errands or just for drives around town. By this time it will be easy to tell whether your dog is a born traveler or would prefer staying at home when you are on the road.

Of course, safety is a concern for dogs in the car. First, he must travel securely, not left loose to roam about the car where he could be injured or distract the driver. A young pup can be held by a passenger initially but should soon graduate to a travel crate, which can be the same crate he uses in the home. Other options include a car harness (like a seat belt for dogs) and partitioning the back of the car with a gate made for this purpose.

Bring along what you will need for the dog. He should wear his collar and ID tags, of course, and you should bring his leash, water (and food if a long trip) and clean-up materials for potty breaks and in case of motion sickness. Always keep your dog on his leash

YOUR PACK ANIMAL

If you are bringing your dog along with you on a vacation, here's a list of the things you want to pack for him:

- leashes (conventional and retractable)
- collar with ID tag
- dog food and bottled water
- grooming tools
- flea and tick sprays
- crate and crate pad
- pooper-scooper and plastic bags
- toys and treats
- towels and paper towels
- first-aid kit
- dog license and rabies certificate

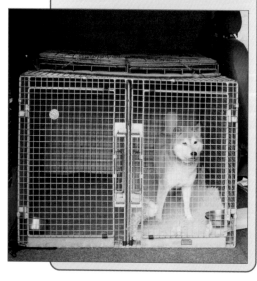

when you make stops, and never leave him alone in the car. Many a dog has died from the heat inside a closed car; this does not take much time at all. A dog left alone inside a car can also be a target for thieves.

DOG-FRIENDLY DESTINATIONS
When planning vacations, a question that often arises is, "Who will watch the dog?" More and more families, however, are answering that question with, "We will!" With the rise in dog-friendly places to visit, the number of families who bring their dogs along on vacation is on the rise. A search online for dog-friendly vacation spots will turn up many choices, as well as resources for owners of canine travelers. Ask others for suggestions: your vet, your breeder, other dog owners, breed club members, people at the local doggie day care.

Traveling with your Shiba Inu means providing for his comfort and safety, and you will have to pack a bag for him just as you do for yourself (although you probably won't have liver treats in your own suitcase!). Bring his everyday items: food, water, bowls, leash and collar (with ID!), brush and comb, toys, bed, crate, plus any additional accessories that he will need once you get to your vacation spot. If he takes

> **DON'T LEAVE HOME WITHOUT IT!**
> For long trips, there's no doubt that the crate is the safest way to travel with your dog. Luckily, there are some other options for owners who can't accommodate a crate in their cars or whose dogs prove exceptionally difficult to crate-train. In some states, seatbelts are mandatory for humans, and you can consider using the seatbelt on your dog. Purchase a safety harness made for passenger pooches and pull your car's seatbelt through the loop on the harness.
>
> You can also consider a car seat made especially for canine passengers. Equipped with their own seatbelts, car seats attach to the seat of the car with the seatbelt.
>
> Likewise, your dog can be restrained in the rear of the vehicle with a barrier, which you can purchase from a pet store or pet-supply outlet. The barrier is constructed of aluminum, steel or mesh netting. While this device will keep the dog in a designated area, it will not protect him from being jostled about the vehicle on a bumpy ride.

medication, don't forget to bring it with you. If going camping or on another type of outdoor excursion, take precautions to protect your dog from ticks, mosquitoes and other pests. Above all, have a good time with your dog and enjoy each other's company!

SHIBA INU

BASIC TRAINING PRINCIPLES: PUPPY VS. ADULT

There's a big difference between training an adult dog and training a young puppy. With a young puppy, everything is new! At eight to ten weeks of age, he will be experiencing many things, and he has nothing with which to compare these experiences. Up to this point, he has been with his

Kabuki responds with enthusiasm and doles out her kisses generously. Training a happy gregarious Shiba proves much easier than one with an aloof or less social temperament.

dam and littermates, not one-on-one with people except in his interactions with his breeder and visitors to the litter.

When you first bring the puppy home, he is eager to please you. This means that he accepts doing things your way. During the next couple of months, he will absorb the basis of everything he needs to know for the rest of his life. This early age is even referred to as the "sponge" stage. After that, for the next 18 months, it's up to you to reinforce good manners by building on the foundation that you've established. Once your puppy is reliable in basic commands and behavior and has reached the appropriate age, you may gradually introduce him to some of the interesting sports, games and activities available to pet owners and their dogs.

Raising your puppy is a family affair. Each member of the family must know what rules to set forth for the puppy and how to use the same one-word commands to mean exactly the same thing every time. Even if yours is a large family, one person will soon be considered by the pup to be the leader, the Alpha person in his pack, the "boss" who must be obeyed. Often that highly regarded person turns out to be the one who feeds the puppy. Food ranks very high on the puppy's list of important things! That's why your puppy is rewarded with small treats along with verbal praise when he responds to you correctly. As the puppy learns to do what you want him to do, the food rewards are gradually eliminated and only the praise remains. If you were to keep up with the food treats, you could have two problems on your hands—an obese dog and a beggar.

Training begins the minute your Shiba Inu puppy steps through the doorway of your home, so don't make the mistake of putting the puppy on the floor and telling him by your actions to "Go for it! Run wild!" Even if this is your first puppy, you must act as if you know what you're doing: be the boss. An uncertain pup may be terrified to move, while a bold one will be ready to take you at your word and start plotting to destroy the house! Before you collected your puppy, you decided where his own special place would be, and that's where to put him when you first arrive home. Give him a house tour after he has investigated his area and had a nap and a bathroom "pit stop."

The key to training a Shiba is consistency—you must commit

OUR CANINE KIDS

"Everything I learned about parenting, I learned from my dog." How often adults recognize that their parenting skills are mere extensions of the education they acquired while caring for their dogs. Many owners refer to their dogs as their "kids" and treat their canine companions like real members of the family. Surveys indicate that a majority of dog owners talk to their dogs regularly, celebrate their dogs' birthdays and purchase Christmas gifts for their dogs. Another survey shows that dog owners take their dogs to the veterinarian more frequently than they visit their own physicians.

and general view of the world.

Working with a professional trainer will speed up your progress with an adopted adult dog. You'll need patience, too. Some new rules may be close to impossible for the dog to accept. After all, he's been successful so far by doing everything his way! (Patience again.) He may agree with your instruction for a few days and then slip back into his old ways, so you must be just as consistent and understanding in your teaching as you would be with a puppy. (More patience needed yet again.) Your dog has to learn to pay attention to your voice, your family, the daily routine, new smells, new sounds

Young puppies, before they reach the age of puberty, are the most impressionable and therefore easier to train. Once the pup begins to rely upon his new owner, instead of his dam, for guidance, he is ready to learn about the world around him.

to the time, set up a schedule and follow it faithfully. Shibas need structure and welcome the regularity of a routine. They do not like monotonous repetition, even for the tastiest treats, and will not repeat a behavior *ad nauseum*, as would a retriever or shepherd.

It's worth mentioning here that, if you've adopted an adult dog that is completely trained to your liking, lucky you! You're off the hook! However, if that dog spent his life up to this point in a kennel, or even in a good home but without any real training, be prepared to tackle the job ahead. A dog three years of age or older with no previous training cannot be blamed for not knowing what he was never taught. While the dog is trying to understand and learn your rules, at the same time he has to unlearn many of his previously self-taught habits

THE RIGHT START

The best advice for a potential dog owner is to start with the very best puppy that money can buy. Don't shop around for a bargain in the newspaper. You're buying a companion, not a used Buick or a second-hand Maytag. The purchase price of the dog represents a very significant part of the investment, but this is indeed a very small sum compared to the expenses of maintaining the dog in good health. If you purchase a well-bred healthy and sound puppy, you will be starting right. An unhealthy puppy can cost you thousands of dollars in unnecessary veterinary expenses and, possibly, a fortune in heartbreak as well.

POTTY COMMAND

Most dogs love to please their masters; there are no bounds to what dogs will do to make their owners happy. The potty command is a good example of this theory. If toileting on command makes the master happy, then more power to him. Puppies will obligingly piddle if it really makes their keepers smile. Some owners can be creative about which word they will use to command their dogs to relieve themselves. Some popular choices are "Potty," "Tinkle," "Piddle," "Let's go," "Hurry up" and "Toilet." Give the command every time your puppy goes into position and the puppy will begin to associate his business with the command.

and, in some cases, even a new climate.

One of the most important things to find out about a newly adopted adult dog is his reaction to children (yours and others), strangers and your friends, and how he acts upon meeting other dogs. If he was not socialized with dogs as a puppy, this could be a major problem. This does not mean that he's a "bad" dog, a vicious dog or an aggressive dog; rather, it means that he has no idea how to read another dog's body language. There's no way for him to tell whether the other dog is a friend or foe. Survival instinct takes over, telling him to

attack first and ask questions later. This definitely calls for professional help and, even then, may not be a behavior that can be corrected 100% reliably (or even at all). If you have a puppy, this is why it is so very important to introduce your young puppy properly to other puppies and "dog-friendly" adult dogs.

HOUSE-TRAINING YOUR SHIBA INU

Dogs are tactility-oriented when it comes to house-training. In other words, they respond to the surface on which they are given approval to eliminate. The choice is yours (the dog's version is in parentheses): The lawn (including the neighbors' lawns)? A bare patch of earth under a tree (where people like to sit and relax in the

The author's partner Robert White with Max, the family Vizsla, and the reluctant Tengu, the author's first Shiba.

Properly house-trained, your Shiba will be reliable in using the approved area for elimination.

signs of improvement will be seen each week. From 8 to 10 weeks old, the puppy will have to be taken outside every time he wakes up, about 10 to 15 minutes after every meal and after every period of play—all day long, from first thing in the morning until his bedtime! That's a total of ten or more trips per day to teach the puppy where it's okay to relieve himself. With that schedule in mind, you can see that house-training a young puppy is not a part-time job. It requires someone to be home all day.

If that seems overwhelming or impossible, do a little planning.

summertime)? Concrete steps or patio (all sidewalks, garage and basement floors)? The curbside (watch out for cars)? A small area of crushed stone in a corner of the yard (mine!)? The latter is the best choice if you can manage it, because it will remain strictly for the dog's use and is easy to keep clean.

You can start out with paper-training indoors and switch over to an outdoor surface as the puppy matures and gains control over his need to eliminate. For the nay-sayers, don't worry—this won't mean that the dog will soil on every piece of newspaper lying around the house. You are training him to go outside, remember? Starting out by paper-training often is the only choice for a city dog.

WHEN YOUR PUPPY'S "GOT TO GO"
Your puppy's need to relieve himself is seemingly non-stop, but

EXTRA! EXTRA!
The headlines read: "Puppy Piddles Here!" Breeders commonly use newspapers to line their whelping pens, so puppies learn to associate newspapers with relieving themselves. Do not use newspapers to line your pup's crate, as this will signal to your puppy that it is OK to urinate in his crate. If you choose to paper-train your puppy, you will layer newspapers on a section of the floor near the door he uses to go outside. You should encourage the puppy to use the papers to relieve himself, and bring him there whenever you see him getting ready to go. Little by little, you will reduce the size of the newspaper-covered area so that the puppy will learn to relieve himself "on the other side of the door."

CANINE DEVELOPMENT SCHEDULE

It is important to understand how and at what age a puppy develops into adulthood.
If you are a puppy owner, consult the following Canine Development Schedule to
determine the stage of development your puppy is currently experiencing.
This knowledge will help you as you work with the puppy in the weeks and months ahead.

PERIOD	AGE	CHARACTERISTICS
FIRST TO THIRD	BIRTH TO SEVEN WEEKS	Puppy needs food, sleep and warmth and responds to simple and gentle touching. Needs mother for security and disciplining. Needs littermates for learning and interacting with other dogs. Pup learns to function within a pack and learns pack order of dominance. Begin socializing pup with adults and children for short periods. Pup begins to become aware of his environment.
FOURTH	EIGHT TO TWELVE WEEKS	Brain is fully developed. Pup needs socializing with outside world. Remove from mother and littermates. Needs to change from canine pack to human pack. Human dominance necessary. Fear period occurs between 8 and 12 weeks. Avoid fright and pain.
FIFTH	THIRTEEN TO SIXTEEN WEEKS	Training and formal obedience should begin. Less association with other dogs, more with people, places, situations. Period will pass easily if you remember this is pup's change-to-adolescence time. Be firm and fair. Flight instinct prominent. Permissiveness and over-disciplining can do permanent damage. Praise for good behavior.
JUVENILE	FOUR TO EIGHT MONTHS	Another fear period about 7 to 8 months of age. It passes quickly, but be cautious of fright and pain. Sexual maturity reached. Dominant traits established. Dog should understand sit, down, come and stay by now.

NOTE: THESE ARE APPROXIMATE TIME FRAMES. ALLOW FOR INDIVIDUAL DIFFERENCES IN PUPPIES.

Get in the habit of walking your Shiba daily, even if you have a fenced yard. For house-training purposes, a daily walk ensures that the owner knows if and when his dog is relieving himself.

HOME WITHIN A HOME

Your Shiba Inu puppy needs to be confined to one secure puppy-proof area when no one is able to watch his every move. Generally the kitchen is the place of choice because the floor is washable. Likewise, it's a busy family area that will accustom the pup to a variety of noises, everything from pots and pans to the telephone, blender and dishwasher. He will also be enchanted by the smell of your cooking (and will never be critical when you burn

For example, plan to pick up your puppy at the start of a vacation period. If you can't get home in the middle of the day, plan to hire a dog-sitter or ask a neighbor to come over to take the pup outside, feed him his lunch and then take him out again about ten or so minutes after he's eaten. Also make arrangements with that or another person to be your "emergency" contact if you have to stay late on the job. Remind yourself—repeatedly—that this hectic schedule improves as the puppy gets older.

DON'T STRESS ME OUT

Your dog doesn't have to deal with paying the bills, the daily commute, PTA meetings and the like, but, believe it or not, there's lots of stress in a dog's world. Stress can be caused by the owner's impatient demeanor and his angry or harsh corrections. If your dog cringes when you reach for his training collar, he's stressed. An older dog is sometimes stressed out when he goes to a new home. No matter what the cause, put off all training until he's over it. If he's going through a fear period—shying away from people, trembling when spoken to, avoiding eye contact or hiding behind furniture—wait to resume training. Naturally you'd also postpone your lessons if the dog were sick, and the same goes for you. Show some compassion.

HOUSE-TRAINING SIGNALS

Watch your puppy for signs that he has to relieve himself (sniffing, circling and squatting), and waste no time in whisking him outside to do his business. Once the puppy is older, you should attach his leash and head for the door. Puppies will always "go" immediately after they wake up, within minutes after eating and after brief periods of play, but young puppies should also be taken out regularly at times other than these, just in case! If necessary, set a timer to remind you to take him out.

something). An exercise pen (also called an "ex-pen," a puppy version of a playpen) within the room of choice is an excellent means of confinement for a young pup. He can see out and has a certain amount of space in which to run about, but he is safe from dangerous things like electrical cords, heating units, trash baskets or open kitchen-supply cabinets. Place the pen where the puppy will not get a blast of heat or air conditioning.

In the pen, you can put a few toys, his bed (which can be his crate if the dimensions of pen and crate are compatible) and a few layers of newspaper in one small corner, just in case. A water bowl can be hung at a convenient height on the side of the ex-pen so it won't become a splashing pool

for an innovative puppy. His food dish can go on the floor, near but not under the water bowl.

Crates are something that pet owners are at last getting used to for their dogs. Wild or domestic canines have always preferred to sleep in den-like safe spots, and that is exactly what the crate provides. How often have you seen adult dogs that choose to sleep under a table or chair even though they have full run of the house? It's the den connection.

In your "happy" voice, use the word "Crate" every time you put the pup into his den. If he's new to a crate, toss in a small biscuit for him to chase the first few times. At night, after he's been outside, he should sleep in his crate. The crate may be kept in his designated area at night or, if you want to be sure to hear those

Establish house rules with your Shiba puppy from the very beginning. This pup has the full run of the house, including sitting on the family sofa. Shibas respond to structure, so make your intentions clear.

Activity naturally triggers the dog's need to relieve himself. After a run around the yard, which in Shiba language we call "the crazies," your dog will need to find a place to relieve himself.

wake-up yips in the morning, put the crate in a corner of your bedroom. However, don't make any response whatsoever to whining or crying. If he's completely ignored, he'll settle down and get to sleep.

Good bedding for a young puppy is an old folded bath towel or an old blanket, something that is easily washable and disposable if necessary ("accidents" will happen!). Never put newspaper in the puppy's crate. Also those old ideas about adding a clock to replace his mother's heartbeat, or a hot-water bottle to replace her warmth, are just that—old ideas. The clock could drive the puppy nuts, and the hot-water bottle could end up as a very soggy waterbed! An extremely good

breeder would have introduced your puppy to the crate by letting two pups sleep together for a couple of nights, followed by several nights alone. How thankful you will be if you found that breeder!

Safe toys in the pup's crate or area will keep him occupied, but monitor their condition closely. Discard any toys that show signs of being chewed to bits. Squeaky parts, bits of stuffing or plastic or any other small pieces can cause intestinal blockage or possibly choking if swallowed.

PROGRESSING WITH POTTY-TRAINING
After you've taken your puppy out and he has relieved himself in the area you've selected, he can have some free time with the family as long as there is someone responsible for watching him. That doesn't mean just someone in the same room who is watching TV or busy on the computer, but one person who is doing nothing other than keeping an eye on the pup, playing with him on the floor and helping him understand his position in the pack.

This first taste of freedom will let you begin to set the house rules. If you don't want the dog on the furniture, now is the time to prevent his first attempts to jump up onto the couch. The word to use in this case is "Off," not "Down." "Down" is the word you will use to teach the down

DAILY SCHEDULE

How many relief trips does your puppy need per day? A puppy up to the age of 14 weeks will need to go outside about 8 to 12 times per day! You will have to take the pup out any time he starts sniffing around the floor or turning in small circles, as well as after naps, meals, games and lessons or whenever he's released from his crate. Once the puppy is 14 to 22 weeks of age, he will require only 6 to 8 relief trips. At the ages of 22 to 32 weeks, the puppy will require about 5 to 7 trips. Adult dogs typically require 4 relief trips per day, in the morning, afternoon, evening and late at night.

position, which is something entirely different.

Most corrections at this stage come in the form of simply distracting the puppy. Instead of telling him "No" for "Don't chew the carpet," distract the chomping puppy with a toy and he'll forget about the carpet.

As you are playing with the pup, do not forget to watch him closely and pay attention to his body language. Whenever you see him begin to circle or sniff, take the puppy outside to relieve himself. If you are paper-training, put him back into his confined area on the newspapers. In either case, praise him as he eliminates while he actually is in the act of relieving himself. Three seconds

after he has finished is too late! You'll be praising him for running toward you, or picking up a toy or whatever he may be doing at that moment, and that's not what you want to be praising him for. Timing is a vital tool in all dog training. Use it!

Remove soiled newspapers immediately and replace them with clean ones. You may want to take a small piece of soiled paper and place it in the middle of the new clean papers, as the scent will attract him to that spot when it's time to go again. That scent attraction is why it's so important to clean up any messes made in the house by using a product specially made to eliminate the odor of dog urine and droppings. Regular household cleansers won't do the trick. Pet shops sell the best pet deodorizers. Invest in

A dog that is trained to relieve herself on grass will always seek out that surface. Adult dogs need to be given access to the relief area about four times a day.

the largest container you can find.

Scent attraction eventually will lead your pup to his chosen spot outdoors; this is the basis of outdoor training. When you take your puppy outside to relieve himself, use a one-word command such as "Outside" or "Go-potty" (that's one word to the puppy!) as you pick him up and attach his leash. Then put him down in his area. If for any reason you can't carry him, snap the leash on quickly and lead him to his spot. Now comes the hard part—hard for you, that is. Just stand there until he urinates and defecates. Move him a few feet in one direction or another if he's just sitting there looking at you, but remember that this is neither playtime nor time for a walk. This is strictly a business trip! Then, as he circles and squats (remember your timing!), give him a quiet "Good dog" as praise. If you start to jump for joy, ecstatic over his performance, he'll do one of two things: either he will stop mid-stream, as it were, or he'll do it again for you—in the house—and expect you to be just as delighted!

Give him five minutes or so and, if he doesn't go in that time, take him back indoors to his confined area and try again in another ten minutes, or immediately if you see him sniffing and circling. By careful observation, you'll soon work out a successful schedule.

> **TIDY BOY**
> Clean by nature, dogs do not like to soil their dens, which in effect are their crates or sleeping quarters. Unless not feeling well, dogs will not defecate or urinate in their crates. Crate training capitalizes on the dog's natural desire to keep his den clean. Be conscientious about giving the puppy as many opportunities to relieve himself outdoors as possible. Reward the puppy for correct behavior. Praise him and pat him whenever he "goes" in the correct location. Even the tidiest of puppies can have potty accidents, so be patient and dedicate more energy to helping your puppy achieve a clean lifestyle.

Accidents, by the way, are just that—accidents. Clean them up quickly and thoroughly, without comment, after the puppy has been taken outside to finish his business and then put back into his area or crate. If you witness an accident in progress, say "No!" in a stern voice and get the pup outdoors immediately. No punishment is needed. You and your puppy are just learning each other's language, and sometimes it's easy to miss a puppy's message. Chalk it up to experience and watch more closely from now on.

KEEPING THE PACK ORDERLY
Discipline is a form of training that brings order to life. For

example, military discipline is what allows the soldiers in an army to work as one. Discipline is a form of teaching and, in dogs, is the basis of how the successful pack operates. Each member knows his place in the pack and all respect the leader, or Alpha dog. It is essential for your puppy that you establish this type of relationship, with you as the Alpha, or leader. It is a form of social coexistence that all canines recognize and accept. Discipline, therefore, is never to be confused with punishment. When you teach your puppy how you want him to behave, and he behaves properly and you praise him for it, you are disciplining him with a form of positive reinforcement.

For a dog, rewards come in the form of praise, a smile, a cheerful tone of voice, a few friendly pats or a rub of the ears. Rewards are also small food treats. Obviously, that does not mean bits of regular dog food. Instead, treats are very small bits of special things like cheese or pieces of soft dog treats. The idea is to reward the dog with something very small that he can taste and swallow, providing instant positive reinforcement. If he has to take time to chew the treat, by the time he is finished he will have forgotten what he did to earn it!

Your puppy should never be physically punished. The displea-

sure shown on your face and in your voice is sufficient to signal to the pup that he has done something wrong. He wants to please everyone higher up on the social ladder, especially his leader, so a scowl and harsh voice will take care of the error. Growling out the word "Shame!" when the pup is caught in the act of doing something wrong is better than the repetitive "No." Some dogs hear "No" so often that they begin to think it's their name! By the way, do not use the dog's

Even as a puppy a Shiba is always on the lookout for potential escape routes.

PUPPY KINDERGARTEN

COLLAR AND LEASH

Before you begin your Shiba Inu puppy's education, he must be used to his collar and leash. Choose a collar for your puppy that is secure, but not heavy or bulky. He won't enjoy training if he's uncomfortable. A flat buckle collar is fine for everyday wear and for initial puppy training. For older dogs, there are several types of training collars such as the martingale, which is a double loop that tightens slightly around the neck, or the head collar, which is similar to a horse's halter. Do not use a chain choke collar unless you have been specifically shown how to put it on and how to use it. You may not be disposed to use a chain choke collar since it can damage the Shiba's coat.

A lightweight 6-foot woven cotton or nylon training leash is preferred by most trainers because it is easy to fold up in your hand and comfortable to hold because there is a certain amount of give

A training collar is effective for the Shiba, but make sure you understand how to use the collar before putting it on your dog.

name when you're correcting him. His name is reserved to get his attention for something pleasant about to take place.

There are punishments that have nothing to do with you. For example, your dog may think that chasing cats is one reason for his existence. You can try to stop it as much as you like but without success, because it's such fun for the dog. But one good hissing, spitting swipe of a cat's claws across the dog's nose will put an end to the game forever. Intervene only when your dog's eyeball is seriously at risk. Cat scratches can cause permanent damage to an innocent but annoying puppy.

> **"SCHOOL" MODE**
> When is your puppy ready for a lesson? Maybe not always when you are. Attempting training with treats just before his mealtime is asking for disaster. Notice what times of day he performs best and make that Fido's school time.

to it. There are lessons where the dog will start off 6 feet away from you at the end of the leash. The leash used to take the puppy outside to relieve himself is shorter because you don't want him to roam away from his area. The shorter leash will also be the one to use when you walk the puppy.

If you've been fortunate enough to enroll in a Puppy Kindergarten Training class, suggestions will be made as to the best collar and leash for your young puppy. I say "fortunate" because your puppy will be in a class with puppies in his age range (up to five months old) of all breeds and sizes. It's the perfect way for him to learn the right way (and the wrong way) to interact with other dogs as well as their people. You cannot teach your puppy how to interpret another dog's sign language. For a first-time puppy owner, these socialization classes are invaluable. For experienced dog owners, they are a real boon to further training.

ATTENTION

You've been using the dog's name since the minute you collected him from the breeder, so you should be able to get his attention by saying his name—with a big smile and in an excited tone of voice. His response will be the puppy equivalent of "Here I am!

> ## LEASH TRAINING
>
> House-training and leash training go hand in hand, literally. When taking your puppy outside to do his business, lead him there on his leash. Unless an emergency potty run is called for, do not whisk the puppy up into your arms and take him outside. If you have a fenced yard, you have the advantage of letting the puppy loose to go out, but it's better to put the dog on the leash and take him to his designated place in the yard until he is reliably house-trained. Taking the puppy for a walk is the best way to house-train a dog. The dog will associate the walk with his time to relieve himself, and the exercise of walking stimulates the dog's bowels and bladder. Dogs that are not trained to relieve themselves on a walk may hold it until they get back home, which of course defeats half the purpose of the walk.

What are we going to do?" Your immediate response (if you haven't guessed by now) is "Good dog." Rewarding him at the moment he pays attention to you teaches him the proper way to respond when he hears his name.

EXERCISES FOR A BASIC CANINE EDUCATION

THE SIT EXERCISE

There are several ways to teach the puppy to sit. The first one is to catch him whenever he is about to sit and, as his backside nears

hand lightly running up his chest, actually lifting his chin up until he sits. Some (usually older) dogs require gentle pressure on their hindquarters with the left hand, in which case the dog should be on your left side. Puppies generally do not appreciate this physical dominance.

After a few times, you should be able to show the dog a treat in the open palm of your hand, raise your hand waist-high as you say "Sit" and have him sit. You thereby have taught him two things at the same time. Both the verbal command and the motion of the hand are signals for the sit. Your puppy is watching you almost more than he is listening to you, so what you do is just as important as what you say.

Don't save any of these drills only for training sessions. Use them as much as possible at odd times during a normal day. The

Practice the sit exercise with your Shiba a few times. Do not torture your Shiba with endless repetitions, or she'll become bored with your routine.

the floor, say "Sit, good dog!" That's positive reinforcement and, if your timing is sharp, he will learn that what he's doing at that second is connected to your saying "Sit" and that you think he's clever for doing it.

Another method is to start with the puppy on his leash in front of you. Show him a treat in the palm of your right hand. Bring your hand up under his nose and, almost in slow motion, move your hand up and back so his nose goes up in the air and his head tilts back as he follows the treat in your hand. At that point, he will have to either sit or fall over, so as his back legs buckle under, say "Sit, good dog," and then give him the treat and lots of praise. You may have to begin with your

> **OKAY!**
> This is the signal that tells your dog that he can quit whatever he was doing. Use "Okay" to end a session on a correct response to a command. (Never end on an incorrect response.) Lots of praise follows. People use "Okay" a lot and it has other uses for dogs, too. Your dog is barking. You say, "Okay! Come!" "Okay" signals him to stop the barking activity and "Come" allows him to come to you for a "Good dog."

dog should always sit before being given his food dish. He should sit to let you go through a doorway first, when the doorbell rings or when you stop to speak to someone on the street.

THE DOWN EXERCISE

Before beginning to teach the down command, you must consider how the dog feels about this exercise. To him, the down is a submissive position. Being flat on the floor with you standing over him is not his idea of fun. It's up to you to let him know that, while it may not be fun, the reward of your approval is worth his effort.

Start with the puppy on your left side in a sit position. Hold the leash right above his collar in your left hand. Have an extra-special treat, such as a small piece of cooked chicken or hotdog, in your right hand. Place it at the end of the pup's nose and steadily move your hand down and forward along the ground. Hold the leash to prevent a sudden lunge for the food. As the puppy goes into the down position, say "Down" very gently.

The difficulty with this exercise is twofold: it's both the submissive aspect and the fact that most people say the word "Down" as if they were a drill sergeant in charge of recruits. So issue the command sweetly, give him the treat and have the pup

When teaching the Shiba to sit, a little pressure on the stubborn end of the dog may give her the idea of what is expected. You can probably teach your Shiba to sit in one or two lessons.

maintain the down position for several seconds. If he tries to get up immediately, place your hands on his shoulders and press down gently, giving him a very quiet "Good dog." As you progress with this lesson, increase the "down time" until he will hold it until you say "Okay" (his cue for release). Practice this one in the house at various times throughout the day.

By increasing the length of time during which the dog must maintain the down position,

More motivated by food than a burning desire to please their owners, Shibas will respond to basic bribes without any injury to their considerable pride. This Shiba doesn't mind the down position as long as she gets to nibble something tasty!

to your original position and offer the reward.

Increase the length of the sit/stay each time until the dog can hold it for at least 30 seconds without moving. After about a week of success, move out on your right foot and take two steps before turning to face the dog. Give the "Stay" hand signal (left palm back toward the dog's head) as you leave. He gets the treat when you return and he holds the sit/stay. Increase the distance that you walk away from him before turning until you reach the length of your training leash. But don't rush it! Go back to the beginning if he moves before he should. No matter what the lesson, never be upset by having to back up for a few days. The repetition and practice are what will make your dog reliable in these commands. It won't do any good to move on to

Once you have accomplished the down command, the down-stay requires little more than the right tone of voice and your Shiba's indulgence.

you'll find many uses for it. For example, he can lie at your feet in the vet's office or anywhere that both of you have to wait, when you are on the phone, while the family is eating and so forth. If you progress to training for competitive obedience, he'll already be all set for the exercise called the "long down."

THE STAY EXERCISE

You can teach your Shiba Inu to stay in the sit, down and stand positions. To teach the sit/stay, have the dog sit on your left side. Hold the leash at waist level in your left hand and let the dog know that you have a treat in your closed right hand. Step forward on your right foot as you say "Stay." Immediately turn and stand directly in front of the dog, keeping your right hand up high so he'll keep his eye on the treat hand and maintain the sit position for a count of five. Return

DOWN

"Down" is a harsh-sounding word and a submissive posture in dog body language, thus presenting two obstacles in teaching the down command. When the dog is about to flop down on his own, tell him "Good down." Pups that are not good about being handled learn better by lowering food in front of them. A dog that trusts you can be gently guided into position. When you give the command "Down," be sure to say it sweetly!

something more difficult if the command is not mastered at the easier levels. Above all, even if you do get frustrated, never let your puppy know! Always keep a positive, upbeat attitude during training, which will transmit to your dog for positive results.

The down/stay is taught in the same way once the dog is completely reliable and steady with the down command. Again, don't rush it. With the dog in the down position on your left side, step out on your right foot as you say "Stay." Return by walking around in back of the dog and into your original position. While you are training, it's okay to murmur something like "Hold on" to encourage him to stay put. When the dog will stay without moving when you are at a distance of 3 or 4 feet, begin to increase the length of time before you return. Be sure he holds the down on your return until you say "Okay." At that point, he gets his treat—just so he'll remember for

next time that it's not over until it's over.

THE COME EXERCISE

No command is more important to the safety of your Shiba Inu than "Come." It is what you should say every single time you see the puppy running toward you: "Kuro, come! Good dog." During playtime, run a few feet away from the puppy and turn and tell him to "Come" as he is already running to you. You can go so far as to teach your puppy two things at once if you squat down and hold out your arms. As the pup gets close to you and

A natural follow-up to the teaching of the sit command is combining that command with the stay command to form the sit/stay—a discipline that will pay off for both you and your Shiba.

you're saying "Good dog," bring your right arm in about waist high. Now he's also learning the hand signal, an excellent device should you be on the phone when you need to get him to come to you! You'll also both be one step ahead when you enter obedience classes.

Puppies, like children, have notoriously short attention spans, so don't overdo it with any of the training. Keep each lesson short. Break it up with a quick run around the yard or a ball toss, repeat the lesson and quit as soon as the pup gets it right. That way, you will always end with a "Good dog."

Hand signals are especially effective on Shibas when there's a liver treat tucked away in your clasped hand. Most Shibas will do anything for a tasty treat.

When the puppy responds to your well-timed "Come," try it with the puppy on the training leash. This time, catch him off guard, while he's sniffing a leaf or watching a bird: "Kuro,

> ### COME AND GET IT!
> The come command is your dog's safety signal. Until he is 99% perfect in responding, don't use the come command if you cannot enforce it. Practice on leash with treats or squeakers, or whenever the dog is running to you. Never call him to come to you if he is to be corrected for a misdemeanor. Reward the dog with a treat and happy praise whenever he comes to you.

come!" You may have to pause for a split second after his name to be sure you have his attention. If the puppy shows any sign of confusion, give the leash a mild jerk and take a couple of steps backward. Do not repeat the command. In this case, you should say "Good come" as he reaches you.

That's the number-one rule of training. Each command word is given just once. Anything more is nagging. You'll also notice that all commands are one word only. Even when they are actually two words, you say them as one.

Never call the dog to come to you—with or without his name— if you are angry or intend to correct him for some misbehavior. When correcting the pup, you go to him. Your dog must always connect "come" with something pleasant and with your approval; then you can rely on his response.

Life isn't perfect and neither are puppies. A time will come, often around 10 months of age, when he'll become "selectively deaf" or choose to "forget" his name. He may respond by wagging his tail (and even seeming to smile at you) with a look that says "Make me!" Laugh, throw his favorite toy and skip the lesson you had planned. Pups will be pups!

THE HEEL EXERCISE

The second most important command to teach, after the come, is the heel. When you are walking your growing puppy, you need to be in control. Besides, it looks terrible to be pulled and yanked down the street, and it's not much fun either. Your eight- to ten-week-old puppy will probably follow you everywhere, but that's his natural instinct, not your control over the situation. However, any time he does follow you, you can say "Heel" and be ahead of the game, as he will learn to associate this command with the action of following you before you even begin teaching him to heel.

There is a very precise, almost military, procedure for teaching your dog to heel. As with all other obedience training, begin with the dog on your left side. He will be in a very nice sit and you will have the training

Stepping out with a young friend, Kabuki loves going on a daily walk. No matter how well heeled the Shiba is, there's always the chance that he'll run away. Be careful when youngsters are walking the dog.

leash across your chest. Hold the loop and folded leash in your right hand. Pick up the slack leash above the dog in your left hand and hold it loosely at your side. Step out on your left foot as you say "Heel." If the puppy does not move, give a gentle tug or pat your left leg to get him started. If he surges ahead of you, stop and pull him back gently until he is at your side. Tell him to sit and begin again.

Walk a few steps and stop while the puppy is correctly

beside you. Tell him to sit and give mild verbal praise. (More enthusiastic praise will encourage him to think the lesson is over.) Repeat the lesson, increasing the number of steps you take only as long as the dog is heeling nicely beside you. When you end the lesson, have him hold the sit, then give him the "Okay" to let him know that this is the end of the lesson. Praise him so that he knows he did a good job.

The cure for excessive pulling (a common problem) is to stop when the dog is no more than 2 or 3 feet ahead of you. Guide him back into position and begin again. With a really determined puller, try switching to a head collar. This will automatically turn the pup's head toward you so you can bring him back easily to the heel position. Give quiet, reassuring praise every time the leash goes slack and he's staying with you.

NO MORE TREATS!

When your dog is responding promptly and correctly to commands, it's time to eliminate treats. Begin by alternating a treat reward with a verbal-praise-only reward. Gradually eliminate all treats while increasing the frequency of praise. Overlook pleading eyes and expectant expressions, but if he's still watching your treat hand, you're on your way to using hand signals.

Staying and heeling can take a lot out of a dog, so provide playtime and free-running exercise to shake off the stress when the lessons are over. You don't want him to associate training with all work and no fun.

TAPERING OFF TIDBITS

Your dog has been watching you—and the hand that treats—throughout all of his lessons, and now it's time to break the treat habit. Begin by giving him treats at the end of each lesson only. Then start to give a treat after the end of only some of the lessons. At the end of every lesson, as well as during the lessons, be consistent with the praise. Your pup now doesn't know whether he'll get a treat or not, but he should keep performing well just in case! Finally, you will stop giving treat rewards entirely. Save them for something brand-new that you want to teach him. Keep up the praise and you'll always have a "good dog."

OBEDIENCE CLASSES

The advantages of an obedience class are that your dog will have to learn amid the distractions of other people and dogs and that your mistakes will be quickly corrected by the trainer. Teaching your dog along with a qualified instructor and other handlers who may have more dog experience than you is another plus of the class environment. The instructor and other handlers can help you to find the most efficient way of teaching your dog a command or exercise. It's often easier to learn from other people's mistakes than your own. You will also learn all of the requirements for competitive obedience trials, in which you can earn titles and go on to advanced jumping and retrieving exercises, which are fun for many dogs. Obedience classes build the foundation needed for many other canine activities (in which we humans are allowed to participate, too!).

TRAINING FOR OTHER ACTIVITIES

Once your dog has basic obedience under his collar and is 12 months of age, you can enter the world of agility training. Dogs think agility is pure fun, like being turned loose in an amusement park full of obstacles. In addition to agility, there are hunting activities for sporting dogs, lure-coursing events for sighthounds, go-to-ground events for terriers, racing for the Nordic sled dogs, herding trials for the shepherd breeds and tracking, which is open to all "nosy" dogs (which would definitely include the Shiba!). For those who like to volunteer, there is the wonderful feeling of owning a Therapy Dog

and visiting hospices, nursing homes and veterans' homes to bring smiles, comfort and companionship to those who live there. Depending on your Shiba's disposition, he may be inclined to meeting strangers. If yours isn't so inclined, he may come around and tolerate some petting.

Around the house, your Shiba Inu can be taught to do some simple chores. You might teach him to carry your socks to the laundry bin (not to his crate) or to fetch the morning newspaper. The kids can teach the dog all kinds of tricks, from playing hide-and-seek to balancing a biscuit on his nose. A family dog is what rounds out the family. Everything he does beyond sitting in your lap or gazing lovingly at you represents the bonus of owning a dog.

THE BEST INVESTMENT

Obedience school is as important for you and your dog as grammar school is for your kids, and it's a lot more fun! Don't shun classes thinking that your dog might embarrass you. He might! Instructors don't expect you to know everything, but they'll teach you the correct way to teach your dog so he won't embarrass you again. He'll become a social animal as you learn with other people and dogs. Home training, while effective in teaching your dog the basic commands, excludes these socialization benefits.

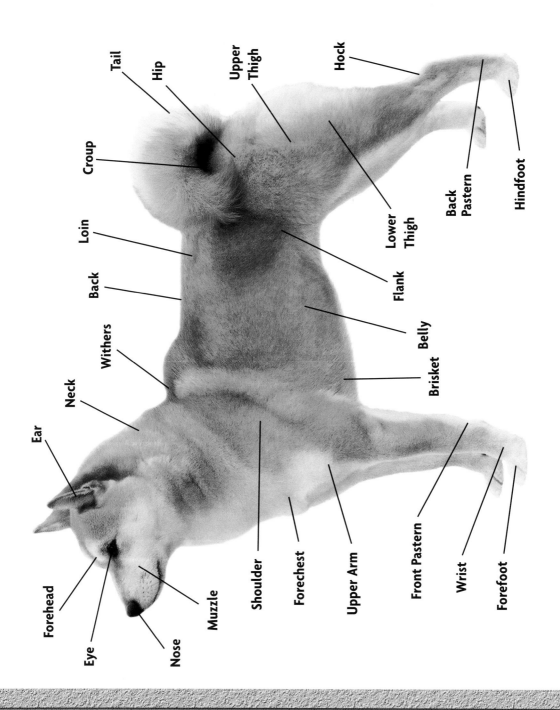

Tail

Hip

Upper Thigh

Hock

Croup

Back Pastern

Hindfoot

Lower Thigh

Loin

Flank

Back

Withers

Belly

Neck

Brisket

Ear

Forehead

Shoulder

Forechest

Upper Arm

Front Pastern

Wrist

Forefoot

Eye

Nose

Muzzle

PHYSICAL STRUCTURE OF THE SHIBA INU

HEALTHCARE FOR YOUR

SHIBA INU

By Lowell Ackerman DVM, DACVD

Your choice of the Shiba Inu offers you many rewards, not the least of which is the breed's hardiness and longevity. There is nothing physically exaggerated about the Shiba, a natural breed that exhibits a near wolf-like form, complete with pointed muzzle, weather-proof plumage and erect, hooded ears. It's not too often a wolf needs a vet, and most Shibas rarely see the vet. The author's veterinarian claims that if all his clients owned Shiba Inus, he would be out of business!

With proper care and veterinary assistance, the Shiba Inu can live to be an active and healthy teenager. The average lifespan of the Shiba is about 13 years, though some lucky Shibas have lived to 17 with consistent good health.

Nonetheless, an owner must be aware of the possible problems that can arise with any dog, even a dog as resilient as the Shiba. It must be mentioned, though, that some Shibas are worriers and, as a result, suffer from recurrent problems. Among the most common of these are ear infections, hot spots (acute moist dermatitis) and inhalant allergies, usually associated with summer grasses and pollen. The well-versed owner is always ready to combat these nuisance problems, which can usually be handled at home.

SELECTING A VETERINARIAN

There is probably no more important decision that you will make regarding your pet's health-care than the selection of his doctor. Your pet's veterinarian will be a pediatrician, family-practice physician and gerontologist, depending on the dog's life stage, and will be the individual who makes recommendations regarding issues such as when specialists need to be consulted, when diagnostic testing and/or therapeutic intervention is needed and when you will need to seek outside emergency and critical-care services. Your vet will act as your healthcare advocate and liaison throughout these processes.

Everyone has his own idea about what to look for in a vet, an individual who will play a big role in his dog's (and, of course, his own) life for many years to come. For some, it is the compassionate caregiver with whom they hope to develop a professional relationship to span the lifetime

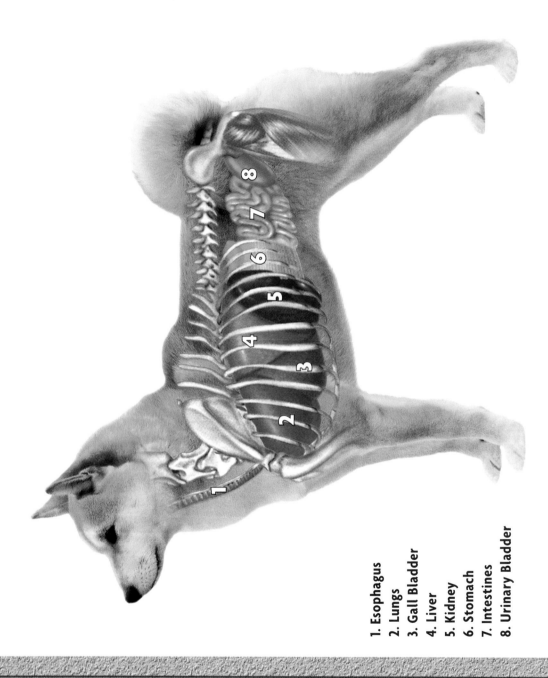

1. Esophagus
2. Lungs
3. Gall Bladder
4. Liver
5. Kidney
6. Stomach
7. Intestines
8. Urinary Bladder

INTERNAL ORGANS OF THE SHIBA INU

of their dogs and even their future pets. For others, they are seeking a clinician with keen diagnostic and therapeutic insight who can deliver state-of-the-art healthcare. Still others need a veterinary facility that is open evenings and weekends, or is in close proximity or provides mobile veterinary services, to accommodate their schedules; these people may not much mind that their dogs might see different veterinarians on each visit. Just as we have different reasons for selecting our own healthcare professionals (e.g., covered by insurance plan, expert in field, convenient location, etc.), we should not expect that there is a one-size-fits-all recommendation for selecting a veterinarian and veterinary practice. The best

advice is to be honest in your assessment of what you expect from a veterinary practice and to conscientiously research the options in your area. You will quickly appreciate that not all veterinary practices are the same, and you will be happiest with one that truly meets your needs.

With all of the opportunities for your Shiba Inu to receive high-quality veterinary medical care, there is another topic that needs to be addressed at the same time—cost. It's been said that you can have excellent healthcare or inexpensive healthcare, but never both; this is as true in veterinary medicine as it is in human medicine. While veterinary costs are a fraction of what the same services cost in the human

THE AGE OF SPECIALISTS

Not that long ago, a single veterinarian would attempt to manage all medical and surgical issues as they arose. That was often problematic, because veterinarians are trained in many species and many diseases, and it was just impossible for general veterinary practitioners to be experts in every species, every field and every ailment. However, just as in the human healthcare fields, specialization has allowed general practitioners to concentrate on primary healthcare delivery, especially wellness and the prevention of infectious diseases, and to utilize a network of specialists to assist in the management of conditions that require specific expertise and experience. Thus there are now many types of veterinary specialists, including dermatologists, cardiologists, ophthalmologists, surgeons, internists, oncologists, neurologists, behaviorists, criticalists and others to help primary-care veterinarians deal with complicated medical challenges. In most cases, specialists see cases referred by primary-care veterinarians, make diagnoses and set up management plans. From there, the animals' ongoing care is returned to their primary-care veterinarians. This important team approach to your pet's medical-care needs has provided opportunities for advanced care and an unparalleled level of quality to be delivered.

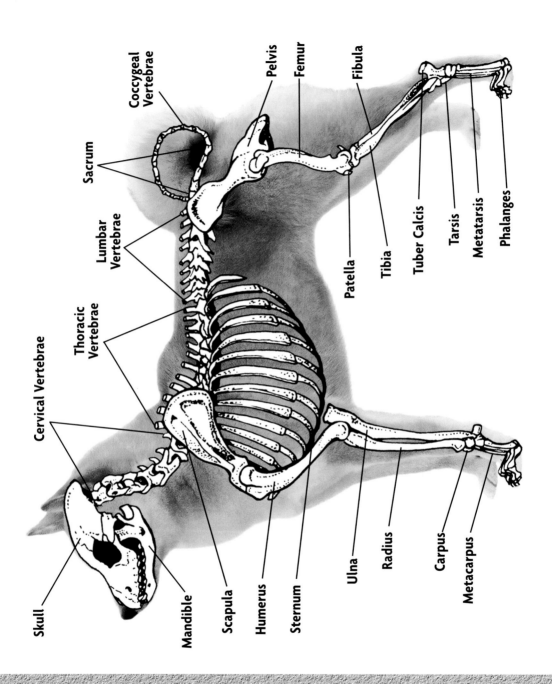

Coccygeal Vertebrae

Sacrum

Pelvis

Femur

Fibula

Lumbar Vertebrae

Patella

Tibia

Tuber Calcis

Tarsis

Metatarsis

Phalanges

Thoracic Vertebrae

Cervical Vertebrae

Skull

Mandible

Scapula

Humerus

Sternum

Ulna

Radius

Carpus

Metacarpus

SKELETAL STRUCTURE OF THE SHIBA INU

healthcare arena, it is still difficult to deal with unanticipated medical costs, especially since they can easily creep into hundreds or even thousands of dollars if specialists or emergency services become involved. However, there are ways of managing these risks. The easiest is to buy pet health insurance and realize that its foremost purpose is not to cover routine healthcare visits but rather to serve as an umbrella for those rainy days when your pet needs medical care and you don't want to worry about whether or not you can afford that care.

VACCINATIONS AND INFECTIOUS DISEASES

There has never been an easier time to prevent a variety of infectious diseases in your dog, but the advances we've made in veterinary medicine come with a price—choice. Now while it may seem that choice is a good thing (and it is), it has never been more difficult for the pet owner (or the veterinarian) to make an informed decision about the best way to protect pets through vaccination.

Years ago, it was just accepted that puppies got a starter series of vaccinations and then annual "boosters" throughout their lives to keep them protected. As more and more vaccines became available, consumers wanted the convenience of having all of that protection in a single injection. The result was "multivalent" vaccines that crammed a lot of protection into a single syringe. The manufacturers' recommendations were to give the vaccines annually, and this was a simple enough protocol to follow. However, as veterinary medicine has become more sophisticated and we have started looking more at healthcare quandaries rather than convenience, it became necessary to reevaluate the situation and deal with some tough questions. It is important to realize that whether or not to use

YOUR SHIBA IN GOOD HANDS

Pet insurance policies are very cost-effective (and very inexpensive by human health-insurance standards), but make sure that you buy the policy long before you intend to use it (preferably starting in puppyhood, because coverage will exclude pre-existing conditions) and that you are actually buying an indemnity insurance plan from an insurance company that is regulated by your state or province. Many insurance policy look-alikes are actually discount clubs that are redeemable only at specific locations and for specific services. An indemnity plan covers your pet at almost all veterinary, specialty and emergency practices and is an excellent way to manage your pet's ongoing healthcare needs.

COMMON INFECTIOUS DISEASES

Let's discuss some of the diseases that create the need for vaccination in the first place. Following are the major canine infectious diseases and a simple explanation of each.

Rabies: A devastating viral disease that can be fatal in dogs and people. In fact, vaccination of dogs and cats is an important public-health measure to create a resistant animal buffer population to protect people from contracting the disease. Vaccination schedules are determined on a government level and are not optional for pet owners; rabies vaccination is required by law in all 50 states.

Parvovirus: A severe, potentially life-threatening disease that is easily transmitted between dogs. There are four strains of the virus, but it is believed that there is significant "cross-protection" between strains that may be included in individual vaccines.

Distemper: A potentially severe and life-threatening disease with a relatively high risk of exposure, especially in certain regions. In very high-risk distemper environments, young pups may be vaccinated with human measles vaccine, a related virus that offers cross-protection when administered at four to ten weeks of age.

Hepatitis: Caused by canine adenovirus type 1 (CAV-1), but since vaccination with the causative virus has a higher rate of adverse effects, cross-protection is derived from the use of adenovirus type 2 (CAV-2), a cause of respiratory disease and one of the potential causes of canine cough. Vaccination with CAV-2 provides long-term immunity against hepatitis, but relatively less protection against respiratory infection.

Canine cough: Also called tracheobronchitis, actually a fairly complicated result of viral and bacterial offenders; therefore, even with vaccination, protection is incomplete. Wherever dogs congregate, canine cough will likely be spread among them. Intranasal vaccination with *Bordetella* and parainfluenza is the best safeguard, but the duration of immunity does not appear to be very long, typically a year at most. These are non-core vaccines, but vaccination is sometimes mandated by boarding kennels, obedience classes, dog shows and other places where dogs congregate to try to minimize spread of infection.

Leptospirosis: A potentially fatal disease that is more common in some geographic regions. It is capable of being spread to humans. The disease varies with the individual "serovar," or strain, of *Leptospira* involved. Since there does not appear to be much cross-protection between serovars, protection is only as good as the likelihood that the serovar in the vaccine is the same as the one in the pet's local environment. Problems with *Leptospira* vaccines are that protection does not last very long, side effects are not uncommon and a large percentage of dogs (perhaps 30%) may not respond to vaccination.

Borrelia burgdorferi: The cause of Lyme disease, the risk of which varies with the geographic area in which the pet lives and travels. Lyme disease is spread by deer ticks in the eastern US and western black-legged ticks in the western part of the country, and the risk of exposure is high in some regions. Lameness, fever and inappetence are most commonly seen in affected dogs. The extent of protection from the vaccine has not been conclusively demonstrated.

Coronavirus: This disease has a high risk of exposure, especially in areas where dogs congregate, but it typically causes only mild to moderate digestive upset (diarrhea, vomiting, etc.). Vaccines are available, but the duration of protection is believed to be relatively short and the effectiveness of the vaccine in preventing infection is considered low.

There are many other vaccinations available, including those for *Giardia* and canine adenovirus-1. While there may be some specific indications for their use, and local risk factors to be considered, they are not widely recommended for most dogs.

a particular vaccine depends on the risk of contracting the disease against which it protects, the severity of the disease if it is contracted, the duration of immunity provided by the vaccine, the safety of the product and the needs of the individual animal. In a very general sense, rabies, distemper, hepatitis and parvovirus are considered core vaccine needs, while parainfluenza, *Bordetella bronchiseptica*, leptospirosis, coronavirus and borreliosis (Lyme disease) are considered non-core needs and best reserved for animals that demonstrate reasonable risk of contracting the diseases.

THE GREAT VACCINATION DEBATE

What kinds of questions need to be addressed? When the vet injects multiple organisms at the same time, might some of the components interfere with one another in the development of immunologic protection? We don't have the comprehensive answer for that question, but it does appear that the immune system better handles agents when given individually. Unfortunately, most manufacturers still bundle their vaccine components because that is what most pet owners want, so getting vaccines with single components can sometimes be difficult.

SAMPLE VACCINATION SCHEDULE

6–8 weeks of age	Parvovirus, Distemper, Adenovirus-2 (Hepatitis)
9–11 weeks of age	Parvovirus, Distemper, Adenovirus-2 (Hepatitis)
12–14 weeks of age	Parvovirus, Distemper, Adenovirus-2 (Hepatitis)
16–20 weeks of age	Rabies
1 year of age	Parvovirus, Distemper, Adenovirus-2 (Hepatitis), Rabies

Revaccination is performed every one to three years, depending on the product, the method of administration and the patient's risk. Initial adult inoculation (for dogs at least 16 weeks of age in which a puppy series was not done or could not be confirmed) is two vaccinations, done three to four weeks apart, with revaccination according to the same criteria mentioned. Other vaccines are given as decided between owner and veterinarian.

Another question has to do with how often vaccines should be given. Again, this seems to be different for each vaccine component. There seems to be a general consensus that a puppy (or a dog with an unknown vaccination history) should get a series of vaccinations to initially stimulate his immunity and then a booster at one year of age, but even the veterinary associations and colleges have trouble reaching agreement about what he should

get after that. Rabies vaccination schedules are not debated, because vaccine schedules for this contagious and devastating disease are determined by government agencies. Regarding the rest, some recommend that we continue to give the vaccines annually because this method has worked well as a disease preventive for decades and delivers predictable protection. Others recommend that some of the vaccines need to be given only every second or third year, as this can be done without affecting levels of protection. This is probably true for some vaccine components (such as hepatitis), but there have been no large studies to demonstrate what the optimal interval should be and whether the same principles hold true for all breeds.

It may be best to just measure titers, which are protective blood levels of various vaccine components, on an annual basis, but that too is not without controversy. Scientists have not precisely determined the minimum titer of specific vaccine components that will be guaranteed to provide a pet with protection. Pets with very high titers will clearly be protected and those with very low titers will need repeat vaccinations, but there is also a large "gray zone" of pets that probably have intermediate protection and may or may

TAKING YOUR DOG'S TEMPERATURE

It is important to know how to take your dog's temperature at times when you think he may be ill. It's not the most enjoyable task, but it can be done without too much difficulty. It's easier with a helper, preferably someone with whom the dog is friendly, so that one of you can hold the dog while the other inserts the thermometer.

Before inserting the thermometer, coat the end with petroleum jelly. Insert the thermometer slowly and gently into the dog's rectum about one inch. Wait for the reading, about two minutes. Be sure to remove the thermometer carefully and clean it thoroughly after each use.

A dog's normal body temperature is between 100.5 and 102.5 degrees F. Immediate veterinary attention is required if the dog's temperature is below 99 or above 104 degrees F.

not need repeat vaccination, depending on their risk of coming into contact with the disease.

These questions leave primary-care veterinarians in a very uncomfortable position, one that is not easy to resolve. Do they recommend annual vaccination in a manner that has demonstrated successful protection for decades, do they recommend skipping vaccines some years and hope that the protection lasts or do they measure blood tests (titers) and hope that the results are convincing enough to clearly indicate whether repeat vaccination is warranted?

These aren't the only vaccination questions impacting pets, owners and veterinarians. Other controversies focus on whether vaccines should be dosed according to body weight (currently they are administered in uniform doses, regardless of the animal's size), whether there are breed-specific issues important in determining vaccination programs (for instance, we know that some breeds have a harder time mounting an appropriate immune response to parvovirus vaccine and might benefit from a different dose or injection interval) and which type of vaccine—live-virus or inactivated—offers more advantages with fewer disadvantages. Clearly, there are many more questions than there are answers. The important thing, as a

pet owner, is to be aware of the issues and be able to work with your veterinarian to make decisions that are right for your pet. Be an informed consumer and you will appreciate the deliberation required in tailoring a vaccination program to best meet the needs of your pet. Expect also that this is an ongoing, ever-changing topic of debate; thus, the decisions you make this year won't necessarily be the same as the ones you make next year.

HOT SPOTS

Shibas, like other double-coated breeds, have a tendency to suffer from hot spots, also known as acute moist dermatitis or pyotraumatic dermatitis. These nuisances usually occur on the dog's side, near his tail or on the tail itself. The dog tends to scratch, lick and bite at a small spot on the coat, which eventually becomes a large open wound. Hot spots frequently accompany flea infestation. It is also possible to develop a hot spot on the cheek or ear, due to an ear infection. Left untreated, a hot

Your breeder should have begun the puppies' vaccination schedule at about six weeks of age. Discuss vaccinations, allergies and skin problems with your breeder to learn his perspective on these concerns for Shibas.

spot can become ulcerated, so owners must tend to them without delay. Your vet is best to handle this so that the hot spot

doesn't become worse over time. It usually requires an injection with a corticosteroid as well as cleaning and shaving the surrounding area. An antibacterial ointment may be applied until the hot spot heals.

In addition to coat problems and ear infections, hot spots can also develop as a result of allergies, including inhalant allergies as well as food or flea allergies. Some breeders believe that hot spots can also be linked to leaving the Shiba's coat wet after a bath. Be sure to dry the dog's coat thoroughly, especially in the rump region and under the tail.

INHALANT ALLERGIES

Shibas can be susceptible to inhalant allergies, which in the past have been called grass allergies, though this is misleading. Dogs can be affected by breathing in various pollens and molds (as well as everyday dust around the house). This leads to itching, which may be year-round (for mold spores and household dust) or seasonal (for weeds, pollen and grasses).

Humans have hay fever, rose fever and other fevers from which they suffer during the pollinating season. Many dogs suffer the same allergies. When the pollen count is high, your dog might suffer, but don't expect him to sneeze and have a runny nose as would a

---

YOUR DOG NEEDS TO VISIT THE VET IF:

- He has ingested a toxin such as antifreeze or a toxic plant; in these cases, administer first aid and call the vet right away
- His teeth are discolored, loose or missing or he has sores or other signs of infection or abnormality in the mouth
- He has been vomiting, has had diarrhea or has been constipated for over 24 hours; call immediately if you notice blood
- He has refused food for over 24 hours
- His eating habits, water intake or toilet habits have noticeably changed; if you have noticed weight gain or weight loss
- He shows symptoms of bloat, which requires immediate attention
- He is salivating excessively
- He has a lump in his throat
- He has a lumps or bumps anywhere on the body
- He is very lethargic
- He appears to be in pain or otherwise has trouble chewing or swallowing
- His skin loses elasticity.

Of course, there will be other instances in which a visit to the vet is necessary; these are just some of the signs that could be indicative of serious problems that need to be caught as early as possible.

Normal hairs of a dog enlarged 200 times original size. The cuticle (outer covering) is clean and healthy. Unlike human hair, which grows from the base, a dog's hair also grows from the end, as shown in the inset.

Most Shiba pups are as resilient and healthy as the tiny fox pups they resemble.

human. Dogs react to pollen allergies the same way they react to fleas—they scratch and bite themselves. Signs of inhalant allergies present themselves around one to three years of age, sometimes as early as six months of age. Scratching can lead to traumatized skin and hot spots. The allergy can be managed with antihistamines and cortisone-based preparations as well as medicated soothing baths.

NEUTERING/SPAYING

Sterilization procedures (neutering for males/spaying for females) are meant to accomplish several purposes. While the underlying premise is to address the risk of pet overpopulation, there are also some medical and behavioral benefits to the surgeries as well. For females, spaying prior to the first estrus (heat cycle) leads to a marked reduction in the risk of mammary cancer. There also will be no manifestations of "heat" to attract male dogs and no bleeding in the house. For males, there is prevention of testicular cancer and a reduction in the risk of prostate problems. In both sexes there may be some limited reduction in aggressive behaviors toward other dogs, and some diminishing of urine marking, roaming and mounting.

While neutering and spaying do indeed prevent animals from contributing to pet overpopulation, even no-cost and low-cost neutering options have not eliminated the problem. Perhaps one of the main reasons for this is that individuals who intentionally breed their dogs and those who allow their animals to run at large are the main causes of unwanted offspring. Also, animals in shelters are often there because they were abandoned or relinquished, not because they came from unplanned matings. Neutering/spaying is important, but it should be considered in the context of the real causes of animals' ending up in shelters and eventually being euthanized.

One of the important considerations regarding neutering is that it is a surgical procedure. This sometimes gets lost in discussions of low-cost procedures and commoditization of the process. In females, spaying is specifically referred to as an ovariohysterectomy. In this procedure, a midline incision is made in the abdomen and the entire uterus and both ovaries are surgically removed. While this is a major invasive surgical procedure, it usually has few complications, because it is typically performed on healthy young animals. However, it is major surgery, as any woman who has had a hysterectomy will attest.

In males, neutering has traditionally referred to castration, which involves the surgical removal of both testicles. While still a significant piece of surgery, there is not the abdominal exposure that is required in the female surgery. In addition, there is now a chemical sterilization option, in which a solution is injected into each testicle, leading to atrophy of the sperm-producing cells. This can typically be done under sedation rather than full anesthesia. This is a relatively new approach, and there are no long-term clinical studies yet available.

Neutering/spaying is typically done around six months of age at most veterinary hospitals, although techniques have been pioneered to perform the procedures in animals as young as eight weeks of age. In general, the surgeries on the very young animals are done for the specific reason of sterilizing them before they go to their new homes. This is done in some shelter hospitals for assurance that the animals will

SPAY'S THE WAY
Although spaying a female dog qualifies as major surgery—an ovariohysterectomy, in fact—this procedure is regarded as routine when performed by a qualified veterinarian on a healthy dog. The advantages to spaying a bitch are many and great. Spayed dogs do not develop uterine cancer or any life-threatening diseases of the genitals. Likewise, spayed dogs are at a significantly reduced risk of breast cancer. Bitches (and owners) are relieved of the demands of heat cycles. A spayed bitch will not leave bloody stains on your furniture during estrus, and you will not have to contend with single-minded macho males trying to climb your fence in order to seduce her. The spayed bitch's coat will not show the ill effects of her estrogen level's climbing such as a dull, lackluster outer coat or patches of hairlessness.

definitely not produce any pups. Otherwise, these organizations need to rely on owners to comply with their wishes to have the animals "altered" at a later date, something that does not always happen.

There are some exciting immunocontraceptive "vaccines" currently under development, and there may be a time when contraception in pets will not require surgical procedures. We anxiously await these developments.

 THE **ABC**s OF
Emergency Care

Abrasions
Clean wound with running water or 3% hydrogen peroxide. Pat dry with gauze and spray with antibiotic. Do not cover.

Animal Bites
Clean area with soap and saline solution or water. Apply pressure to any bleeding area. Apply antibiotic ointment.

Antifreeze Poisoning
Induce vomiting and take dog to the vet.

Bee Sting
Remove stinger and apply soothing lotion or cold compress; give antihistamine in proper dosage.

Bleeding
Apply pressure directly to wound with gauze or towel for five to ten minutes. If wound does not stop bleeding, wrap wound with gauze and adhesive tape.

Bloat/Gastric Torsion
Immediately take the dog to the vet or emergency clinic; phone from car. No time to waste.

Burns
Chemical: Bathe dog with water and pet shampoo. Rinse in saline solution. Apply antibiotic ointment.

Acid: Rinse with water. Apply one part baking soda, two parts water to affected area.

Alkali: Rinse with water. Apply one part vinegar, four parts water to affected area.

Electrical: Apply antibiotic ointment. Seek veterinary assistance immediately.

Choking
If the dog is on the verge of collapsing, wedge a solid object, such as the handle of screwdriver, between molars on one side of the mouth to keep mouth open. Pull tongue out. Use long-nosed pliers or fingers to remove foreign object. Do not push the object down the dog's throat. For small or medium dogs, hold dog upside down by hind legs and shake firmly to dislodge foreign object.

Chlorine Ingestion
With clean water, rinse the mouth and eyes. Give the dog water to drink; contact the vet.

Constipation
Feed dog 2 tablespoons bran flakes with each meal. Encourage drinking water. Mix 1/4 teaspoon mineral oil in dog's food.

Diarrhea
Withhold food for 12 to 24 hours. Feed dog anti-diarrheal with eyedropper. When feeding resumes, feed one part boiled hamburger, one part plain cooked rice, 1/4 to 3/4 cup four times daily.

Dog Bite
Snip away hair around puncture wound; clean with 3% hydrogen peroxide; apply tincture of iodine. If wound appears deep, take the dog to the vet.

Frostbite
Wrap the dog in a heavy blanket. Warm affected area with a warm bath for ten minutes. Red color to skin will return with circulation; if tissues are pale after 20 minutes, contact the vet.

Use a portable, durable container large enough to contain all items

Heat Stroke
Partially submerge the dog in cold water; if no response within ten minutes, contact the vet.

Hot Spots
Mix 2 packets Domeboro® with 2 cups water. Saturate cloth with mixture and apply to hot spots for 15 to 30 minutes. Apply antibiotic ointment. Repeat every six to eight hours.

Poisonous Plants
Wash affected area with soap and water. Cleanse with alcohol. For foxtail/grass, apply antibiotic ointment.

Rat Poison Ingestion
Induce vomiting. Keep dog calm, maintain dog's normal body temperature (use blanket or heating pad). Get to the vet for antidote.

Shock
Keep the dog calm and warm; call for veterinary assistance.

Snake Bite
If possible, bandage the area and apply pressure. If the area is not conducive to bandaging, use ice to control bleeding. Get immediate help from the vet.

Tick Removal
Apply flea and tick spray directly on tick. Wait one minute. Using tweezers or wearing plastic gloves, apply constant pull while grasping tick's body. Apply antibiotic ointment.

Vomiting
Restrict dog's water intake; offer a few ice cubes. Withhold food for next meal. Contact vet if vomiting persists longer than 24 hours.

DOG OWNER'S FIRST-AID KIT
- ❑ **Gauze bandages/swabs**
- ❑ **Adhesive and non-adhesive bandages**
- ❑ **Antibiotic powder**
- ❑ **Antiseptic wash**
- ❑ **Hydrogen peroxide 3%**
- ❑ **Antibiotic ointment**
- ❑ **Lubricating jelly**
- ❑ **Rectal thermometer**
- ❑ **Nylon muzzle**
- ❑ **Scissors and forceps**
- ❑ **Eyedropper**
- ❑ **Syringe**
- ❑ **Anti-bacterial/fungal solution**
- ❑ **Saline solution**
- ❑ **Antihistamine**
- ❑ **Cotton balls**
- ❑ **Nail clippers**
- ❑ **Screwdriver/pen knife**
- ❑ **Flashlight**
- ❑ **Emergency phone numbers**

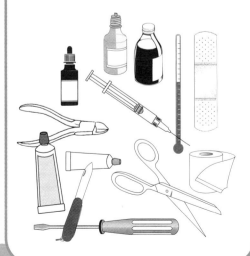

A scanning electron micrograph of a dog flea, Ctenocephalides canis, on dog hair.

EXTERNAL PARASITES

FLEAS

Fleas have been around for millions of years and, while we have better tools now for controlling them than at any time in the past, there still is little chance that they will end up on an endangered species list. Actually, they are very well adapted to living on our pets, and they continue to adapt as we make advances.

The female flea can consume 15 times her weight in blood during active reproduction and can lay as many as 40 eggs a day. These eggs are very resistant to the effects of insecticides. They hatch into larvae, which then pupate and spin cocoons. The immature fleas reside in this pupal stage until the time is right for feeding. This pupal stage is also very resistant to the effects of insecticides, and pupae can last in the environment without feeding for many months. Newly emergent fleas are attracted to animals by the warmth of the animals' bodies, movement and exhaled carbon dioxide. However, when they first emerge from their cocoons, they orient towards light; thus when an animal passes between a flea and the light source, casting a shadow, the flea pounces and starts to feed. If the animal turns out to be a dog or cat, the reproductive cycle continues. If the flea lands on another type of animal, including a person, the flea will bite but will then look for a more appropriate host. An emerging adult flea can survive without feeding for up to 12 months but, once it tastes blood, it can survive off its host for only three to four days.

It was once thought that fleas spend most of their lives in the environment, but we now know that fleas won't willingly jump off a dog unless leaping to another dog or when physically removed by brushing, bathing or other manipulation. Flea eggs, on the other hand, are shiny and smooth, and they roll off the animal and into the environment. The eggs, larvae and pupae then exist in the environment, but once the adult finds a susceptible animal, it's home sweet home until the flea is forced to seek refuge elsewhere.

Since adult fleas live on the animal and immature forms survive in the environment, a successful treatment plan must address all stages of the flea life cycle. There are now several safe and effective flea-control products that can be applied on a monthly

> ## FLEA PREVENTION FOR YOUR DOG
> - Discuss with your veterinarian the safest product to protect your dog, likely in the form of a monthly tablet or a liquid preparation placed on the back of the dog's neck.
> - For dogs suffering from flea-bite dermatitis, a shampoo or topical insecticide treatment is required.
> - Your lawn and property should be sprayed with an insecticide designed to kill fleas and ticks that lurk outdoors.
> - Using a flea comb, check the dog's coat regularly for any signs of parasites.
> - Practice good housekeeping. Vacuum floors, carpets and furniture regularly, especially in the areas that the dog frequents, and wash the dog's bedding weekly.
> - Follow up house-cleaning with carpet shampoos and sprays to rid the house of fleas at all stages of development. Insect growth regulators are the safest option.

basis. These include fipronil, imidacloprid, selamectin and permethrin (found in several formulations). Most of these products have significant flea-killing rates within 24 hours. However, none of them will control the immature forms in the environment. To accomplish this, there are a variety of insect growth regulators that can be sprayed into

THE FLEA'S LIFE CYCLE

What came first, the flea or the egg? This age-old mystery is more difficult to comprehend than the actual cycle of the flea. Fleas usually live only about four months. A female can lay 2,000 eggs in her lifetime.

Egg

After ten days of rolling around your carpet or under your furniture, the eggs hatch into larvae, which feed on various and sundry debris. In days or months, depending on the climate, the larvae spin cocoons and develop into the pupal or nymph stage, which quickly develop into fleas.

Larva

Pupa

These immature fleas must locate a host within 10 to 14 days or they will die. Only about 1% of the flea population exist as adult fleas, while the other 99% exist as eggs, larvae or pupae.

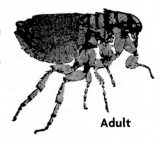

Adult

KILL FLEAS THE NATURAL WAY

If you choose not to go the route of conventional medication, there are some natural ways to ward off fleas:

- Dust your dog with a natural flea powder, composed of such herbal goodies as rosemary, wormwood, pennyroyal, citronella, rue, tobacco powder and eucalyptus.
- Apply diatomaceous earth, the fossilized remains of single-cell algae, to your carpets, furniture and pet's bedding. Even though it's not good for dogs, it's even worse for fleas, which will dry up swiftly and die.
- Brush your dog frequently, give him adequate exercise and let him fast occasionally. All of these activities strengthen the dog's system and make him more resistant to disease and parasites.
- Bathe your dog with a capful of pennyroyal or eucalyptus oil.
- Feed a natural diet, free of additives and preservatives. Add some fresh garlic and brewer's yeast to the dog's morning portion, as these items have flea-repelling properties.

the environment (e.g., pyriprox-yfen, methoprene, fenoxycarb) as well as insect development inhibitors such as lufenuron that can be administered. These compounds have no effect on adult fleas, but they stop immature forms from developing into adults. In years gone by we relied heavily on toxic insecticides (such as organophosphates, organochlorines and carbamates) to manage the flea problem, but today's options are not only much safer to use on our pets but also safer for the environment.

TICKS

Ticks are members of the spider class (arachnids) and are blood-sucking parasites capable of transmitting a variety of diseases, including Lyme disease, ehrlichiosis, babesiosis and Rocky Mountain spotted fever. It's easy to see ticks on your own skin, but it is more of a challenge when your treasured dog is affected. Whenever you happen to be planning a stroll in a tick-infested area (especially forests, grassy or wooded areas or parks) be prepared to do a thorough inspection of your dog afterward to search for ticks. Ticks can be tricky, so make sure you spend time looking in the ears, between the toes and everywhere else where a tick might hide. Ticks need to be attached for 24–72 hours before they transmit most of the diseases that they carry, so you do have a window of opportunity for some preventive intervention.

Female ticks live to eat and

S. E. M. by PHOTOTAKE.

A scanning electron micrograph of the head of a female deer tick, *Ixodes dammini*, a parasitic tick that carries Lyme disease.

breed. They can lay between 4,000 and 5,000 eggs and they die soon after. Males, on the other hand, live only to mate with the females and continue the process as long as they are able. Most ticks live on multiple hosts before parasitizing dogs. The immature forms typically reside on grass and shrubs, waiting for susceptible animals to walk by. The larvae and nymph stages typically feed on wildlife.

If only a few ticks are present on a dog, they can be plucked out, but it is important to remove the entire head and mouthparts,

---

A TICKING BOMB

There is nothing good about a tick's harpooning his nose into your dog's skin. Among the diseases caused by ticks are Rocky Mountain spotted fever, canine ehrlichiosis, canine babesiosis, canine hepatozoonosis and Lyme disease. If a dog is allergic to the saliva of a female wood tick, he can develop tick paralysis.

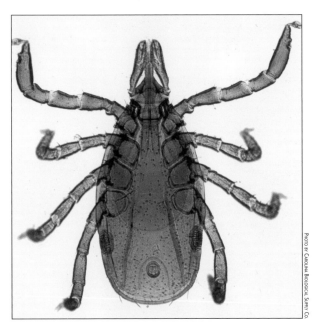

Deer tick,
Ixodes dammini.

PHOTO BY CAROLINA BIOLOGICAL SUPPLY CO.

disposed of in a container of alcohol or household bleach.

Some of the newer flea products, specifically those with fipronil, selamectin and permethrin, have effect against some, but not all, species of tick. Flea collars containing appropriate pesticides (e.g., propoxur, chlorfen-vinphos) can aid in tick control. In most areas, such collars should be placed on animals in March, at the beginning of the tick season, and changed regularly. Leaving the collar on when the pesticide level is waning invites the development of resistance. Amitraz collars are also good for tick control, and the active ingredient does not interfere with other flea-control products. The ingredient helps prevent the attachment of ticks to the skin and will cause those ticks already on the skin to detach themselves.

which may be deeply embedded in the skin. This is best accomplished with forceps designed especially for this purpose; fingers can be used but should be protected with rubber gloves, plastic wrap or at least a paper towel. The tick should be grasped as closely as possible to the animal's skin and should be pulled upward with steady, even pressure. Do not squeeze, crush or puncture the body of the tick or you risk exposure to any disease carried by that tick. Once the ticks have been removed, the sites of attachment should be disinfected. Your hands should then be washed with soap and water to further minimize risk of contagion. The tick should be

TICK CONTROL

Removal of underbrush and leaf litter and the thinning of trees in areas where tick control is desired are recommended. These actions remove the cover and food sources for small animals that serve as hosts for ticks. With continued mowing of grasses in these areas, the probability of ticks' surviving is further reduced. A variety of insecticide ingredients (e.g., resmethrin, carbaryl, permethrin, chlorpyrifos, dioxathion and allethrin) are registered for tick control around the home.

MITES

Mites are tiny arachnid parasites that parasitize the skin of dogs. Skin diseases caused by mites are referred to as "mange," and there are many different forms seen in dogs. These forms are very different from one another, each one warranting an individual description.

Sarcoptic mange, or scabies, is one of the itchiest conditions that affects dogs. The microscopic *Sarcoptes* mites burrow into the superficial layers of the skin and can drive dogs crazy with itchiness. They are also communicable to people, although they can't complete their reproductive cycle on people. In addition to being tiny, the mites also are often difficult to find when trying to make a diagnosis. Skin scrapings from multiple areas are examined microscopically but, even then, sometimes the mites cannot be found.

Fortunately, scabies is relatively easy to treat, and there are a variety of products that will successfully kill the mites. Since the mites can't live in the environment for very long without feeding, a complete cure is usually possible within four to eight weeks.

Cheyletiellosis is caused by a relatively large mite, which sometimes can be seen even without a microscope. Often referred to as "walking dandruff," this also causes itching, but not usually as profound as with scabies.

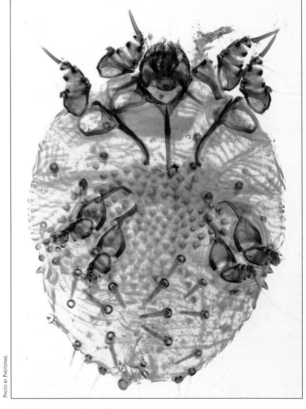

PHOTO BY PHOTOTAKE.

While *Cheyletiella* mites can survive somewhat longer in the environment than scabies mites, they too are relatively easy to treat, being responsive to not only the medications used to treat scabies but also often to flea-control products.

Otodectes cynotis is the canine ear mite and is one of the more common causes of mange, especially in young dogs in shelters or pet stores. That's because the mites are typically present in large numbers and are quickly spread to

Sarcoptes scabiei, commonly known as the "itch mite."

Micrograph of a dog louse, *Heterodoxus spiniger.* Female lice attach their eggs to the hairs of the dog. As the eggs hatch, the larval lice bite and feed on the blood. Lice can also feed on dead skin and hair. This feeding activity can cause hair loss and skin problems.

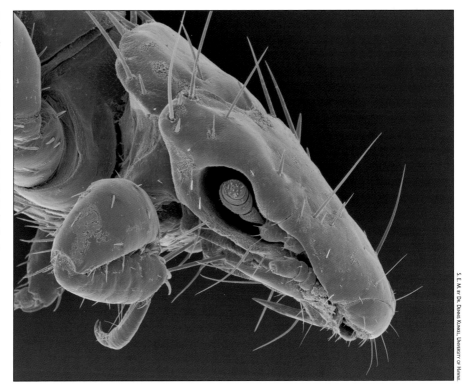

S. E. M. BY DR. DENNIS KUNKEL, UNIVERSITY OF HAWAII

nearby animals. The mites rarely do much harm but can be difficult to eradicate if the treatment regimen is not comprehensive. While many try to treat the condition with ear drops only, this is the most common cause of treatment failure. Ear drops cause the mites to simply move out of the ears and as far away as possible (usually to the base of the tail) until the insecticide levels in the ears drop to an acceptable level—then it's back to business as usual! The successful treatment of ear mites requires treating all animals in the household with a systemic insecti-cide, such as selamectin, or a

combination of miticidal ear drops combined with whole-body flea-control preparations.

Demodicosis, sometimes referred to as red mange, can be one of the most difficult forms of mange to treat. Part of the problem has to do with the fact that the mites live in the hair follicles and they are relatively well shielded from topical and systemic products. The main issue, however, is that demodectic mange typically results only when there is some underlying process interfering with the dog's immune system.

Since *Demodex* mites are

normal residents of the skin of mammals, including humans, there is usually a mite population explosion only when the immune system fails to keep the number of mites in check. In young animals, the immune deficit may be transient or may reflect an actual inherited immune problem. In older animals, demodicosis is usually seen only when there is another disease hampering the immune system, such as diabetes, cancer, thyroid problems or the use of immune-suppressing drugs. Accordingly, treatment involves not only trying to kill the mange mites but also discerning what is interfering with immune function and correcting it if possible.

Chiggers represent several different species of mite that don't parasitize dogs specifically, but do latch on to passersby and can cause irritation. The problem is most prevalent in wooded areas in the late summer and fall. Treatment is not difficult, as the mites do not complete their life cycle on dogs and are susceptible to a variety of miticidal products.

MOSQUITOES

Mosquitoes have long been known to transmit a variety of diseases to people, as well as just being biting pests during warm weather. They also pose a real risk to pets. Not only

do they carry deadly heartworms but recently there also has been much concern over their involvement with West Nile virus. While we can avoid heartworm with the use of preventive medications, there are no such preventives for West Nile virus. The only method of prevention in endemic areas is active mosquito control. Fortunately, most dogs that have been exposed to the virus only developed flu-like symptoms and, to date, there have not been the large number of reported deaths in canines as seen in some other species.

Illustration of *Demodex folliculoram.*

ILLUSTRATION BY PHOTOTAKE

MOSQUITO REPELLENT

Low concentrations of DEET (less than 10%), found in many human mosquito repellents, have been safely used in dogs but, in these concentrations, probably give only about two hours of protection. DEET may be safe in these small concentrations, but since it is not licensed for use on dogs, there is no research proving its safety for dogs. Products containing permethrin give the longest-lasting protection, perhaps two to four weeks. As DEET is not licensed for use on dogs, and both DEET and permethrin can be quite toxic to cats, appropriate care should be exercised. Other products, such as those containing oil of citronella, also have some mosquito-repellent activity, but typically have a relatively short duration of action.

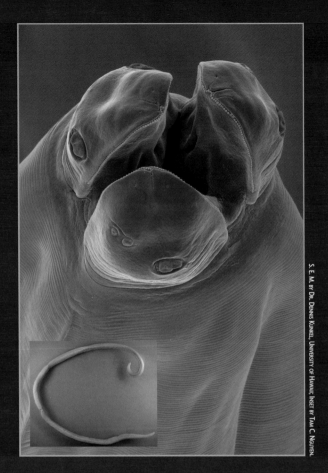

S. E. M. BY DR. DENNIS KUNKEL, UNIVERSITY OF HAWAII; INSET BY TAM C. NGUYEN.

The ascarid roundworm *Toxocara canis,* showing the mouth with three lips. INSET: Photomicrograph of the roundworm *Ascaris lumbricoides.*

INTERNAL PARASITES: WORMS

ASCARIDS

Ascarids are intestinal roundworms that rarely cause severe disease in dogs. Nonetheless, they are of major public health significance because they can be transferred to people. Sadly, it is children who are most commonly affected by the parasite, probably from inadvertently ingesting ascarid-contaminated soil. In fact, many yards and children's sandboxes contain appreciable numbers of ascarid eggs. So, while ascarids don't bite dogs or latch onto their intestines to suck blood, they do cause some nasty medical conditions in children and are best eradicated from our furry friends. Because pups can start passing ascarid eggs by three weeks of age, most parasite-control programs begin at two weeks of age and are repeated every two weeks until pups are eight weeks old. It is important to

HOOKED ON *ANCYLOSTOMA*

Adult dogs can become infected by the bloodsucking nematodes we commonly call hookworms via ingesting larvae from the ground or via the larvae penetrating the dog's skin. It is not uncommon for infected dogs to show no symptoms of hookworm infestation. Sometimes symptoms occur within ten days of exposure. These symptoms can include bloody diarrhea, anemia, loss of weight and general weakness. Dogs pass the hookworm eggs in their stools, which serves as the vet's method of identifying the infestation. The hookworm larvae can encyst themselves in the dog's tissues and be released when the dog is experiencing stress.

Caused by an *Ancylostoma* species whose common host is the dog, cutaneous larval migrans affects humans, causing itching and lumps and streaks beneath the surface of the skin.

S. E. M. BY DR. DENNIS KUNKEL, UNIVERSITY OF HAWAII

realize that bitches can pass ascarids to their pups even if they test negative prior to whelping. Accordingly, bitches are best treated at the same time as the pups.

HOOKWORMS

Unlike ascarids, hookworms do latch onto a dog's intestinal tract and can cause significant loss of blood and protein. Similar to ascarids, hookworms can be transmitted to humans, where they cause a condition known as cutaneous larval migrans. Dogs can become infected either by consuming the infective larvae or by the larvae's penetrating the skin directly. People most often get infected when they are lying on the ground (such as on a beach) and the larvae penetrate the skin. Yes, the larvae can penetrate through a beach blanket. Hookworms are typically susceptible to the same medications used to treat ascarids.

The hookworm *Ancylostoma caninum* infests the intestines of dogs. INSET: Note the row of teeth at the posterior end, used to anchor the worm to the intestinal wall.

WHIPWORMS

Whipworms latch onto the lower aspects of the dog's colon and can cause cramping and diarrhea. Eggs do not start to appear in the dog's feces until about three months after the dog was infected. This worm has a peculiar life cycle, which makes it more difficult to control than ascarids or hookworms. The good thing is that whipworms rarely are transferred to people.

Some of the medications used to treat ascarids and hookworms are also effective against whipworms, but, in general, a separate treatment protocol is needed. Since most of the medications are effective against the adults but not the eggs or larvae, treatment is typically repeated in three weeks, and then often in three

WORM-CONTROL GUIDELINES

• Practice sanitary habits with your dog and home.
• Clean up after your dog and don't let him sniff or eat other dogs' droppings.
• Control insects and fleas in the dog's environment. Fleas, lice, cockroaches, beetles, mice and rats can act as hosts for various worms.
• Prevent dogs from eating uncooked meat, raw poultry and dead animals.
• Keep dogs and children from playing in sand and soil.
• Kennel dogs on cement or gravel; avoid dirt runs.
• Administer heartworm preventives regularly.
• Have your vet examine your dog's stools at your annual visits.
• Select a boarding kennel carefully so as to avoid contamination from other dogs or an unsanitary environment.
• Prevent dogs from roaming. Obey local leash laws.

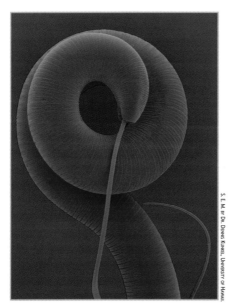

Adult whipworm, *Trichuris* sp., an intestinal parasite.

S.E.M. BY DR. DENNIS KUNKEL, UNIVERSITY OF HAWAII.

months as well. Unfortunately, since dogs don't develop resistance to whipworms, it is difficult to prevent them from getting reinfected if they visit soil contaminated with whipworm eggs.

TAPEWORMS

There are many different species of tapeworm that affect dogs, but *Dipylidium caninum* is probably the most common and is spread by fleas. Flea larvae feed on organic debris and tapeworm eggs in the environment and, when a dog chews at himself and manages to ingest fleas, he might get a dose of tapeworm at the same time. The tapeworm then develops further in the intestine of the dog.

The tapeworm itself, which latches onto the intestinal wall, is composed of numerous segments. When the segments break off into the intestine (as proglottids), they may accumulate around the rectum, like grains of rice. While this tapeworm is disgusting in its behavior, it is not directly communicable to humans (although humans can also get infected by swallowing fleas).

A much more dangerous flatworm is *Echinococcus multilocularis*, which is typically found in foxes, coyotes and wolves. The eggs are passed in the feces and infect rodents, and, when dogs eat the rodents, the dogs can be infected by thousands of adult tapeworms. While the parasites don't cause many problems in dogs, this is considered the most lethal worm infection that people can get. Take appropriate precautions if you live in an area in which these tapeworms are found. Do not use mulch that may contain feces of dogs, cats or wildlife, and discourage your pets from hunting wildlife. Treat these tapeworm

infections aggressively in pets, because if humans get infected, approximately half die.

HEARTWORMS

Heartworm disease is caused by the parasite *Dirofilaria immitis* and is seen in dogs around the world. A member of the roundworm group, it is spread between dogs by the bite of an infected mosquito. The mosquito injects infective larvae into the dog's skin with its bite, and these larvae develop under the skin for a period of time before making their way to the heart. There they develop into adults, which grow and create blockages of the heart, lungs and major blood vessels there. They also start producing offspring (microfilariae)

A dog tapeworm proglottid (body segment).

The dog tapeworm *Taenia pisiformis*.

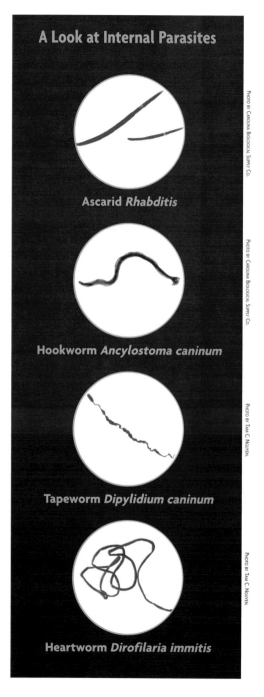

A Look at Internal Parasites

Ascarid *Rhabditis*

PHOTO BY CAROLINA BIOLOGICAL SUPPLY CO.

Hookworm *Ancylostoma caninum*

PHOTO BY CAROLINA BIOLOGICAL SUPPLY CO.

Tapeworm *Dipylidium caninum*

PHOTO BY TAM C. NGUYEN.

Heartworm *Dirofilaria immitis*

PHOTO BY TAM C. NGUYEN.

and these microfilariae circulate in the bloodstream, waiting to hitch a ride when the next mosquito bites. Once in the mosquito, the microfilariae develop into infective larvae and the entire process is repeated.

When dogs get infected with heartworm, over time they tend to develop symptoms associated with heart disease, such as coughing, exercise intolerance and potentially many other manifestations. Diagnosis is confirmed by either seeing the microfilariae themselves in blood samples or using immunologic tests (antigen testing) to identify the presence of adult heartworms. Since antigen tests measure the presence of adult heartworms and microfilarial tests measure offspring produced by adults, neither are positive until six to seven months after the initial infection. However, the beginning of damage can occur by fifth-stage larvae as early as three months after infection. Thus it is possible for dogs to be harboring problem-causing larvae for up to three months before either type of test would identify an infection.

The good news is that there are great protocols available for preventing heartworm in dogs. Testing is critical in the process, and it is important to understand the benefits as well as the limitations of such testing. All dogs six months of age or older that have not been on continuous heartworm-preventive medication should be

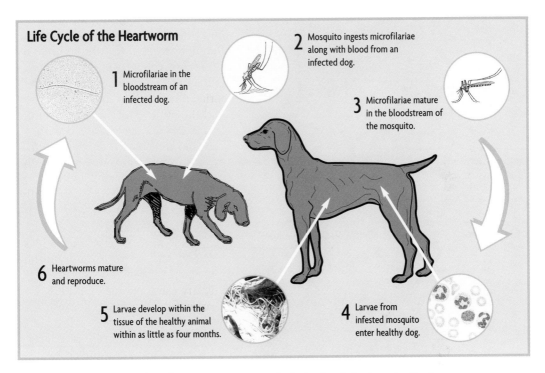

Life Cycle of the Heartworm

1 Microfilariae in the bloodstream of an infected dog.

2 Mosquito ingests microfilariae along with blood from an infected dog.

3 Microfilariae mature in the bloodstream of the mosquito.

4 Larvae from infested mosquito enter healthy dog.

5 Larvae develop within the tissue of the healthy animal within as little as four months.

6 Heartworms mature and reproduce.

screened with microfilarial or antigen tests. For dogs receiving preventive medication, periodic antigen testing helps assess the effectiveness of the preventives. The American Heartworm Society guidelines suggest that annual retesting may not be necessary when owners have absolutely provided continuous heartworm prevention. Retesting on a two- to three-year interval may be sufficient in these cases. However, your veterinarian will likely have specific guidelines under which heartworm preventives will be prescribed, and many prefer to err on the side of safety and retest annually.

It is indeed fortunate that heartworm is relatively easy to prevent, because treatments can be as life-threatening as the disease itself. Treatment requires a two-step process that kills the adult heartworms first and then the microfilariae. Prevention is obviously preferable; this involves a once-monthly oral or topical treatment. The most common oral preventives include ivermectin (not suitable for some breeds), moxidectin and milbemycin oxime; the once-a-month topical drug selamectin provides heartworm protection in addition to flea, tick and other parasite controls.

Is dog showing in your blood? Are you excited by the idea of gaiting your handsome Shiba Inu around the ring to the thunderous applause of an enthusiastic audience? Are you certain that your beloved Shiba Inu is flawless? You are not alone! Every loving owner thinks that his dog has no faults, or too few to mention. No matter how many times an owner reads the breed standard, he cannot find any faults in his noble companion dog. If this sounds like you, and if you are considering entering your Shiba Inu in a dog show, here are some basic questions to ask yourself:

- Did you purchase a "show-quality" puppy from the breeder?
- Is your puppy at least six months of age?

- Does the puppy exhibit correct show type for his breed?
- Does your puppy have any disqualifying faults?
- Is your Shiba Inu registered with the American Kennel Club?
- How much time do you have to devote to training, grooming, conditioning and exhibiting your dog?
- Do you understand the rules and regulations of a dog show?
- Do you have time to learn how to show your dog properly?
- Do you have the financial resources to invest in showing your dog?
- Will you show the dog yourself or hire a professional handler?
- Do you have a vehicle that can accommodate your weekend trips to the dog shows?

Success in the show ring requires more than a pretty face, a waggy tail and a pocketful of liver. Even though dog shows can be exciting and enjoyable, the sport of conformation makes great demands on the exhibitors and the dogs. Winning exhibitors live for their dogs, devoting time and money to their dogs' presentation, conditioning and training. Very few novices, even those with good

Ch. Katuranishiki of Oikawa House, or "Chibi" for short, is a top American sire who passed on his exquisite head, type and movement to many great dogs. Chibi is the sire of the author's dog, Jacquet's Tengu, bred by Richard Tomita.

dogs, will find themselves in the winners' circle, though it does happen. Don't be disheartened, though. Every exhibitor began as a novice and worked his way up to the Group ring. It's the "working your way up" part that you must keep in mind.

Assuming that you have purchased a puppy of the correct type and quality for showing, let's begin to examine the world of showing and what's required to get started. Although the entry fee into a dog show is nominal, there are lots of other hidden costs involved with "finishing" your Shiba Inu, that is, making him a champion. Things like equipment, travel, training and conditioning all cost money. A more serious campaign will include fees for a professional handler, boarding, cross-country travel and advertising. Top-winning show dogs can represent a very considerable investment— over $100,000 has been spent in campaigning some dogs. (The investment can be less, of course, for owners who don't use professional handlers.)

Many owners, on the other hand, enter their "average" Shiba Inus in dog shows for the fun and enjoyment of it. Dog showing makes an absorbing hobby, with many rewards for dogs and owners alike. If you're having fun, meeting other people who share your interests and enjoying the overall experience, you likely will catch

SEAL OF EXCELLENCE

The show ring is the testing ground for a breeder's program. A championship on a dog signifies that three qualified judges have placed their seal of approval on that dog. Only dogs that have earned their championships should be considered for breeding purposes. Striving to improve the breed and reproduce sound, typical examples of the breed, breeders must breed only the best. No breeder breeds only for pet homes; they strive for the top. The goal of every program must be to better the breed, and every responsible breeder wants the prestige of producing Best in Show winners.

the "bug." Once the dog-show bug bites, its effects can last a lifetime; it's certainly much better than a deer tick! Soon you will be envisioning yourself in the center ring at the Westminster Kennel Club Dog Show in New York City, competing for the prestigious Best in Show cup. This magical dog show is televised annually from Madison Square Garden, and the victorious dog becomes a celebrity overnight.

AKC CONFORMATION SHOWING

GETTING STARTED
Visiting a dog show as a spectator is a great place to start. Pick up the show catalog to find out what time your breed is being shown, who is judging the breed and in

How your dog compares to the breed standard, in the judge's opinion, is the basis for a conformation show. Your Shiba must be trained to stand properly, gait on lead and accept the judge's inspection.

which ring the classes will be held. To start, Shiba Inus compete against other Shiba Inus, and the winner is selected as Best of Breed by the judge. This is the procedure for each breed. At a Group show, all of the Best of Breed winners go on to compete for Group One in their respective group. For example, Best of Breed winners in the Non-Sporting Group compete against each other; this is done for all seven groups. Finally, all seven Group winners go head to head in the ring for the Best in Show award.

What most spectators don't understand is the basic idea of conformation. A dog show is often referred as a "conformation" show. This means that the judge should decide how each dog stacks up (conforms) to the breed standard for his given breed: how well does this Shiba Inu conform to the ideal representative detailed in the standard? Ideally, this is what happens. In reality, however, this ideal often gets slighted as the judge compares Shiba Inu #1 to Shiba Inu #2. Again, the ideal is that each dog is judged based on his merits in comparison to his breed standard, not in comparison to the other dogs in the ring. It is easier for judges to compare dogs of the same breed to decide which they think is the better specimen; in the Group and Best in Show ring, however, it is very difficult to compare one breed to another, like apples to oranges. Thus the dog's conformation to the breed standard—not to mention advertising dollars and good handling—is essential to success in conformation shows. The dog described in the standard (the standard for each AKC breed is written and approved by the breed's national parent club and then submitted to the AKC for approval) is the perfect dog of that breed, and breeders keep their eye on the standard when they choose which dogs to breed, hoping to get closer and closer to the ideal with each litter.

Another good first step for the novice is to join a dog club. You will be astonished by the many and different kinds of dog clubs in the country, with about 5,000 clubs holding events every year. Most clubs require that prospective new members present two letters of recommendation from existing members. Perhaps you've made some friends visiting a show held by a particular club and you would like to join that club. Dog clubs may specialize in a single breed, like a local or regional Shiba Inu club, or in a specific pursuit, such as obedience, tracking or hunting tests. There are all-breed clubs for all-dog enthusiasts; they sponsor special training days, seminars on topics like grooming or handling or lectures on breeding or canine genetics. There are also clubs that specialize in certain types of dogs,

Many Shibas are natural show dogs, intuitive of their God-given grace and beauty. Not every Shiba is this easy to handle in the ring!

like herding dogs, hunting dogs, companion dogs, etc.

A parent club is the national organization, sanctioned by the AKC, which promotes and safeguards its breed in the country. The National Shiba Club of America was formed in 1983 and can be contacted on the Internet at www.shiba.org. The parent club holds an annual national specialty show, usually in a different city each year, in which many of the country's top dogs, handlers and breeders gather to compete. At a specialty show, only members of a single breed are invited to participate. There are also Group specialties, in which all members of a Group are invited. For more information about dog clubs in your area, contact the AKC at www.akc.org on the Internet or write them at 5580 Centerview Drive, Raleigh, NC 27606.

HOW SHOWS ARE ORGANIZED

Three kinds of conformation shows are offered by the AKC. There is the all-breed show, in which all AKC-recognized breeds can compete, the single-breed specialty show and the Group show.

For a dog to become an AKC champion of record, the dog must earn 15 points at shows. The points must be awarded by at least three different judges and must include two "majors" under different judges. A "major" is a three-, four- or five-point win, and the number of points per win is determined by the number of dogs competing in the show on that day. (Dogs that are absent or are excused are not counted.) The number of points that are awarded varies from breed to breed. More dogs are needed to attain a major in more popular breeds, and fewer dogs are needed in less popular breeds. Yearly, the AKC evaluates the number of dogs in competition in each division (there are 14 divisions in all, based on geography) and may or may not change the numbers of dogs required for each number of points.

Only one dog and one bitch of each breed can win points at a given show. There are no "co-ed" classes except for champions of record. Dogs and bitches do not compete against each other until they are champions. Dogs that are not champions (referred to as "class dogs") compete in one of five classes. The class in which a dog is entered depends on age and previous show wins. First there is the Puppy Class (sometimes divided further into classes for 6- to 9-month-olds and 9- to 12-month-olds); next is the Novice Class (for dogs that have no points toward their championship and whose only first-place wins have come in the Puppy Class or the Novice Class, the latter class limited to three first places); then there is the American-bred Class (for dogs bred in the US); the Bred-by-Exhibitor Class (for dogs handled by their breeders or by immediate family members of their breeders) and the Open Class (for any non-champions). Any dog may enter the Open class, regardless of age or win history, but to be competitive the dog should be older and have ring experience.

EXPRESS YOURSELF
The most intangible of all canine attributes, expression speaks to the character of the breed, attained by the combined features of the head. The shape and balance of the dog's skull, the color and position of the eyes and the size and carriage of the head mingle to produce the correct expression of the breed. A judge may approach a dog and determine instantly whether the dog's face portrays the desired impression for the breed, conveying nobility, intelligence and alertness among other specifics of the breed standard.

The judge at the show begins judging the male dogs in the Puppy Class(es) and proceeds through the other classes. The judge awards first through fourth place in each class. The first-place winners of each class then compete with one another in the Winners Class to determine Winners Dog. The judge then starts over with the bitches, beginning with the Puppy Class(es) and proceeding up to the Winners Class to award Winners Bitch, just as he did with the dogs. A Reserve Winners Dog and Reserve Winners Bitch are also selected; they could be awarded the points in the case of a disqualification.

The Winners Dog and Winners Bitch are the two that are awarded the points for their breed. They then go on to compete with any champions of record (often called "specials") of their breed that are entered in the show. The champions may be dogs or bitches; in this class, all are shown together. The judge reviews the Winners Dog and Winners Bitch along with all of the champions to select the Best of Breed winner. The Best of Winners is selected between the Winners Dog and Winners Bitch; if one of these two is selected Best of Breed as well, he or she is automatically determined Best of Winners. Lastly, the judge selects Best of Opposite Sex to the Best of Breed winner. The Best of Breed winner then goes on to the Group competition.

At a Group or all-breed show, the Best of Breed winners from each breed are divided into their respective groups to compete against one another for Group One through Group Four. Group One (first place) is awarded to the dog that best lives up to the ideal for his breed as described in the standard. A Group judge, therefore, must have a thorough working knowledge of many breed standards. After placements have been made in each Group, the seven Group One winners (from the Sporting Group, Toy Group, Hound Group, etc.) compete against each other for the top honor, Best in Show.

UNDERSTANDING THE CANINE MINDSET

You and your dog are on different wavelengths. Your dog is similar to a toddler in that both live in the present tense only. A dog's view of life is based primarily on cause and effect.

Your dog makes connections based on the fact that he lives in the present, so when he is doing something and you interrupt to dispense praise or a correction, a connection, positive or negative, is made. To the dog, that's like one plus one equals two! In the same sense, it's also easy to see that when your timing is off, you will cause an incorrect connection. The one-plus-one way of thinking is why you must never scold a dog for behavior that took place an hour, 15 minutes or even 15 seconds ago. But it is also why, when your timing is perfect, you can teach him to do all kinds of wonderful things—as soon as he has made that essential connection. What helps the process is his desire to please you and to have your approval.

There are behaviors we admire in dogs, such as friendliness and obedience, as well as those behaviors that cause problems to a varying degree. The dog owner who encounters minor behavioral problems is wise to solve them promptly or get professional help. Bad behaviors are not corrected by repeatedly shouting "No" or getting angry with the dog. Only the giving of praise and approval for good behavior lets your dog understand right from wrong. The longer a bad behavior is allowed to continue, the harder it is to overcome. A responsible breeder is often able to help. Each

Decoding the Shiba mind is akin to curing the common cold: a riddle that cannot be solved. Looking into the eyes of a Shiba certainly assures us humans that this is a very intelligent breed of dog.

LOOK AT ME WHEN I SPEAK TO YOU

Your dog considers direct eye contact as a sign of dominance. A shy dog will avoid looking at you; a dominant dog will try to stare you down. What you want is for your dog to pay attention when you speak, and that doesn't necessarily involve direct eye contact. In dealing with a problem dog, avert your gaze momentarily, return to face the dog and give an immediate down command. Show him that you're the boss.

dog is unique, so try not to compare your dog's behavior with your neighbor's dog or the one you had as a child.

Have your veterinarian check the dog to see whether a behavior problem could have a physical cause. An earache or toothache, for example, could be the reason for a dog to snap at you if you were to touch his head when putting on his leash. A sharp correction from you would only increase the behavior. When a physical basis is eliminated, and if the problem is not something you understand or can cope with, ask for the name of a behavioral specialist, preferably one who is familiar with the Shiba. Be sure to keep the breeder informed of your progress.

Many things, such as environment and inherited traits, form

the basic behavior of a dog, just as in humans. You also must factor into his temperament the purpose for which your dog was originally bred. The major obstacle lies in the dog's inability to explain his behavior to us in a way that we understand. The one thing you should not do is to give up and abandon your dog. Somewhere a misunderstanding has occurred but, with help and patient understanding on your part, you should be able to work out the majority of bothersome behaviors.

AGGRESSION

"Aggression" is a word that is often misunderstood and is sometimes even used to describe what is actually normal canine behavior. For example, it's normal for puppies to growl when playing tug-of-war. It's puppy talk. There are different forms of dog aggression, but all are degrees of dominance, indicating that the dog, not his master, is (or thinks he is) in control. When the dog feels that he (or his control of the situation) is threatened, he will respond. The extent of the aggressive behavior varies with individual dogs. It is not at all pleasant to see bared teeth or to hear your Shiba growl or snarl, but these are signs of behavior that, if left uncorrected, can become extremely dangerous. A word of warning here: never challenge an aggressive dog. He is unpredictable and therefore unreliable to approach.

Nothing gets a "hello" from strangers on the street quicker than walking a puppy, but people should ask permission before petting your dog so you can tell him to sit in order to receive the admiring pats. If a hand comes down over the dog's head and he shrinks back, ask the person to bring his hand up, underneath the pup's chin. Now you're correcting strangers, too! But if you don't, it could make your dog afraid of strangers, which in turn can lead to fear-biting. Socialization prevents much aggression before it rears its ugly head.

The body language of an aggressive dog about to attack is clear. The dog will have a hard, steady stare. He will try to look as big as possible by standing stiff-legged, pushing out his chest, keeping his ears up and holding his tail up and steady. The hackles on his back will rise so that a ridge of hairs stands up. This posture may include the curled lip, snarl and/or growl, or he may be silent. He looks, and definitely is, very dangerous.

This dominant posture is seen in dogs that are territorially aggressive. Deliverymen are constant victims of serious bites from such dogs. Territorial aggression is the reason you should never, ever, try to train a puppy to be a watchdog. It can escalate into

this type of behavior over which you will have no control. All forms of aggression must be taken seriously and dealt with immediately. If signs of aggressive behavior continue, or grow worse, or if you are at all unsure about how to deal with your dog's behavior, get the help of a professional.

Uncontrolled aggression, sometimes called "irritable aggression," is not something for the pet owner to try to solve. If you cannot solve your dog's dangerous behavior with professional help, and you (quite rightly) do not wish to keep a canine time-bomb in your home, you will have some important decisions to make. Aggressive dogs often cannot be rehomed successfully, as they are dangerous and unreliable in their behavior. An aggressive dog should be dealt with only by someone who knows exactly the situation that he is getting into and has the experience, dedication and ideal living environment to attempt rehabilitating the dog, which often is not possible. In these cases, the dog ends up having to be humanely put down. Making a decision about euthanasia is not an easy undertaking for anyone, for any reason, but you cannot pass on to another home a dog that you know could cause harm.

A milder form of aggression is the dog's guarding anything that he perceives to be his—his food dish, his toys, his bed and/or his crate. This can be prevented if you take firm control from the start. The young puppy can and should be taught that his leader will share, but that certain rules apply. Guarding is mild aggression only in the beginning stages, and it will worsen and become dangerous if you let it.

Don't try to snatch anything away from your puppy. Bargain for the item in question so that you can positively reinforce him when he gives it up. Punishment only results in worsening any aggressive behavior.

Many dogs extend their guarding impulse toward items they've stolen. The dog figures, "If I have it, it's mine!" (Some ill-behaved kids have similar tendencies.) An angry confrontation will only increase the dog's aggression. (Have you ever watched a child have a tantrum?) Try a simple distraction first, such as tossing a toy or picking up his leash for a walk. If that doesn't work, the best way to handle the situation is with basic obedience. Show the dog a treat, followed by calm, almost slow-motion commands: "Come. Sit. Drop it. Good dog," and then hand over the cheese. That's one example of positive-reinforcement training.

Children can be bitten when they try to retrieve a stolen shoe or toy, so they need to know how to handle the dog or to let an adult do it. They may also be bitten as they run away from a dog, in either fear or play. The dog sees the child's running as reason for pursuit, and even a friendly young puppy will nip at the heels of a runaway. Teach the kids not to run away from a strange dog and when to stop overly exciting play with their own puppy.

CHEWING

All puppies chew. All dogs chew. This is a fact of life for canines, and sometimes you may think it's what your dog does best. A pup starts chewing when his first set of teeth erupts and continues throughout the teething period. Chewing gives the pup relief from itchy gums and incoming teeth and, from that time on, he gets great satisfaction out of this normal, somewhat idle, canine activity. Providing safe chew toys is the best way to direct this behavior in an appropriate

Puppies will chew anything...until they are scolded. Be firm and fair when reprimanding your misbehaving Shiba puppy and you will gain his respect.

manner. Chew toys are available in all sizes, textures and flavors, but you must monitor the wear-and-tear inflicted on your pup's toys to be sure that the ones you've chosen are safe and remain in good condition.

Puppies cannot distinguish between a rawhide toy and a nice leather shoe or wallet. It's up to you to keep your possessions away from the dog and to keep your eye on the dog. There's a form of destruction caused by chewing that is not the dog's fault. Let's say you allow him on the sofa. One day he takes a rawhide bone up on the sofa and, in the course of chewing on the bone, takes up a bit of fabric. He continues to chew. Disaster! Now you've learned the lesson: dogs with chew toys have to be either kept off furniture and carpets, carefully supervised or put into their confined areas for chew time.

The wooden legs of furniture are favorite objects for chewing. The first time, tell the dog "Leave it!" (or "No!") and offer him a chew toy as a substitute. But your clever dog may be hiding under the chair and doing some silent destruction, which you may not notice until it's too late. In this case, it's time to try one of the foul-tasting products, made specifically to prevent destructive chewing, that is sprayed on the objects of your dog's chewing

> ## CURES FOR COMMON BOREDOM
> Dogs are social animals that need company. Lonely and tied-out dogs bark, hoping that someone will hear them. Prevent this from happening by never tying your dog out in the yard and giving him the attention that he needs. If you don't, then don't blame the dog. Bored dogs will think up clever ways to overcome their boredom. Digging is a common diversion for a dog left alone outside for too long. The remedy is to bring him indoors or put a layer of crushed stone in his confined outdoor area. If you catch him in the act of "gardening," it requires immediate correction. Keep your dog safe by embedding the fencing about a foot or more below ground level to foil a would-be escape artist.

attention. These products also work to keep the dog away from plants, trash, etc. It's even a good way to stop the dog from "mouthing" or chewing on your hands or the leg of your pants. (Be sure to wash your hands after the mouthing lesson!) A little spray goes a long way.

DIGGING
Digging is another natural and normal doggy behavior. Wild canines dig to bury whatever food they can save for later to eat. (And you thought *we* invented the doggy bag!) Burying bones or toys

is a primary cause to dig. Dogs also dig to get at interesting little underground creatures like moles and mice. In the summer, they dig to get down to cool earth. In winter, they dig to get beneath the cold surface to warmer earth.

The solution to the last two is easy. In the summer, provide a bed that's up off the ground and placed in a shaded area. In winter, the dog should either be indoors to sleep or given an adequate insulated doghouse outdoors. To understand how natural and normal this is for Shibas you have only to consider the Nordic breeds of sled dog who, at the end of the run, routinely dig a bed for themselves in the snow. It's the nesting instinct. How often have you seen your dog go round and round in circles, pawing at his blanket or bedding before flopping down to sleep?

For Shibas, digging may have less to do with nature than it has to do with escape! Most Shibas practice their digging— conveniently—next to a fence. A persistent Shiba can easily dig a hole deep enough to get under a fence to run away. When your Shiba shows signs of digging to escape, it's time for an owner to take real precautions to prevent the dog's disappearance.

Digging to escape is a lot more dangerous than it is destructive. A dog that digs under the fence is

Owners must take precautions with fertilizers and pesticides when treating flowers in their garden. The curious Shiba will taste-test almost everything in her path.

the one that is hit by a car or becomes lost. A good fence to protect a digger should be set 10 to 12 inches below ground level, and every fence needs to be routinely checked for even the smallest openings can become possible escape routes.

Catching your dog in the act of digging is the easiest way to stop it, because your dog will make the one-plus-one connection, but digging is too often a solitary occupation, something the lonely dog does out of boredom. Catch your young puppy in the act and put a stop to it before you have a yard full of craters.

FOOD-RELATED PROBLEMS

We're not talking about eating, diets or nutrition here, we're talking about bad habits. Face it. All dogs are beggars. Food is the motivation for everything we want our dogs to do and, when you combine that with their innate ability to "con" us in order to get their way, it's a wonder there aren't far more obese dogs in the world.

Who can resist the bleeding-heart look that says "I'm starving," or the paw that gently pats your knee and gives you a knowing look, or the whining "please" or even the total body language of a perfect sit beneath the cookie jar. No one who professes to love his dog can turn down the pleas of his clever Shiba's performances every time. One thing is for sure though: definitely do not allow begging at the table. Family meals do not include your dog.

Control your dog's begging habit by making your dog work for his rewards. Ignore his begging when you can. Utilize the obedience commands you've taught your dog. Use "Off" for the pawing. A sit or even a long down will interrupt the whining. His reward in these situations is definitely not a treat. Casual verbal praise is enough. Be sure all members of the family follow the same rules. There is a different type of begging that does demand your immediate response and that is the appeal to be let (or taken) outside. Usually that is a quick paw or small whine to get your attention, followed by a race to the door. This type of begging needs your quick attention and approval. Of course, a really smart dog will soon figure out how to cut you off at the pass and direct you to that cookie jar on your way to the door. Some dogs are always one step ahead of us.

Stealing food is a problem only if you are not paying attention. A dog can't steal food that is not within his reach. Leaving your dog in the kitchen with the roast beef on the table is asking for trouble. Nothing idiopathic about this problem, though perhaps a little idiotic! Putting cheese and crackers on the coffee table also requires a watchful eye to stop the thief in

Human food is much more tasty than dry dog food, so Shibas are poised and professional beggars. To prevent your dog from begging at the table, never feed him from the table (even once!).

Speed, timing and careful planning are required to steal food from the garbage can. Kabuki has been perfecting her techniques since puppyhood.

food. Stealing food from the garbage is an age-old penchant of the Shiba, and one which the breed does with professional ease. On occasion my Shibas have actually opened the fridge while I was not at home and helped themselves to a belly-bursting meal. One time the two Shibas actually dragged an entire turkey from the top shelf of the fridge and left a very sad carcass in the middle of the kitchen floor. Reprimanding them did no good whatsoever, as they seemingly didn't recognize the ravaged bird and were too tired to become concerned. Another time, the dynamic duo broke into the fridge to steal three pounds of baked livers, which I had prepared for bait for the following day's dog show. The iron-enriched Shibas had absolutely no interest in a liver treat the next day at the show and kept looking away from me as if to say, "Stop it please, you're nauseating me!"

his tracks. The word to use (one word, remember, even if it's two words pronounced as one) is "Leave it!" Instead of preceding it with yet another "No," try using a guttural sound like "Aagh!" That sounds more like a warning growl to the dog and therefore has instant meaning.

Canine thieves are in their element when little kids are carrying cookies in their hands! Your dog will think he's been exceptionally clever if he causes a child to drop a cookie. Bonanza! The easiest solution is to keep dog and children separated at snack time. You must also be sure that the children understand that they must not tease the dog with food—his or theirs. Your dog does not mean to bite the kids, but when he snatches at a tidbit so near the level of his mouth, it can result in an unintended nip.

The author's Shibas have proven remarkably inventive in their plots to steal food. As you know, Shibas love to eat and are always ready for a taste of human

The allure of the litterbox! If your Shiba acquires the taste for feline feces, there may be something lacking in her diet.

INDEX

My Shiba Inu

PUT YOUR PUPPY'S FIRST PICTURE HERE

Dog's Name _____

Date _____ Photographer _____